Unethical

Lauren Biel

Copyright © 2023 by Lauren Biel

All rights reserved.

No part of this book may be reproduced in any form or by any electronic or mechanical means, including information storage and retrieval systems, without written permission from the author, except for the use of brief quotations in a book review.

This is a work of fiction. Names, characters, events, and incidents are the products of the author's imagination. Any resemblance to actual persons, living or dead, or actual events is purely coincidental.

Library of Congress Cataloging-in-Publication Data

Unethical/Lauren Biel 1st ed.

Cover Design: DesignbyCharlyy

Editing: Sugar Free Editing

Interior Design: Sugar Free Editing

For more information on this book and the author, visit: www.LaurenBiel.com

Please visit LaurenBiel.com for a full list of content warnings.

This book is dedicated to the good girls who think stalkers are just a little misunderstood

Chapter One

Maxim

An electrical whirring comes from behind me as the door closes and locks. I'm free, even if I don't really think I should be free at all. Bad people like me shouldn't walk around with normal people with normal brains. But I'm really good at blending in. I can meld with the worst of the criminals and the most mundane of society. I just made a stupid mistake and got caught this time.

I've murdered people, but the law has remained completely blind to those offenses. The stolen car was what hemmed me up. And then I maybe caused a little fight with the officer who tried to apprehend me.

Now they say I need therapy. I don't think I need therapy for my anger, but it might help with everything else that's wrong with my brain. The thought of talking about my feelings makes me more homicidal than it should, though.

I study the paperwork once more and follow the directions to the halfway house, where I'll stay until I finish therapy and get a job, because that's so easy to do as a felon. I cross through the city on foot, heading toward the building that's almost guaranteed to be a dump. My gaze returns to the paperwork as I walk, just to keep my mind on something other than the stifling heat rising from the pavement.

Though I didn't receive a death sentence, this is almost as bad. I can't drink or do drugs, and I'm forced to check in every night by ten p.m. The random piss tests are just the sprinkles on this shit sundae. The whole thing sounds awfully shitty.

I eye the paperwork again and spot the therapist's name at the bottom. Dr. Sarah Reeves. I've spent the last four years in prison, so I can only hope she's a gray-haired bat with a sharp nose. I'm not sure how well I can hold myself back if she's hot. Self-control isn't a strength of mine. Dangle a hot piece of ass in front of me, and I might fuck the judgement out of her.

Curiosity gets the better of me. I pull out the cheapo phone the prison gave me and type her name into the browser. My jaw tightens when her picture appears on the screen. She *is* hot. And I'll have to sit in front of her and pretend I'm not rabid for pussy at this point. More specifically, *her* pussy.

Fuck, I guess I'll go. Maybe I'll even like it. She might not, though. That depends on how much she pries into my mind. I can only hope she has a flashlight if she chooses to venture into a darkness she's not prepared for. All the schooling in the world won't help her once she delves into my pitch-black depths. My fucked-up brain.

Who knows, though? Most mental-health providers have a darkness of their own. Their own problems inspire their career choice. No one understands fucked-up like those who are also a bit fucked.

Unethical

Just a week until my first appointment, and then we'll see just how well the prison therapy will help me control my impulses. I don't have much hope, especially considering the impulses I'm getting after seeing her picture.

Maybe a visit with the doctor won't be so bad after all.

Chapter Two

Sarah

I come into work and sit down at my desk. A paper glares up at me from the smooth oak surface. I pick it up and see that the court has assigned a new client to me. Great.

These are my least favorite types of clients. Instead of choosing to seek help on their own, they've been forced to meet some psychiatric quota for a problem they refuse to acknowledge. Or worse, a problem they acknowledge and refuse to change.

They don't want to be here. They often have little interest in bettering themselves because they don't think anything is wrong with them. The world has wronged *them*, not the other way around. There's little worse than sitting across from a smug ex-con who thinks the entire justice system is out to get them.

What do you even talk about with patients like that? It's usually clear as day that there *is* something wrong with them. The justice system is out to get them because they need to be gotten, and most of them should still be in prison because they haven't made the progress needed to integrate successfully back into society.

But the prisons and jails are too overcrowded, so here we are.

His name is Maxim Jankowski. His intimidating first name creates a vision in my mind. Tall. Tattooed. Scary. I'm pretty certain there's a serial killer with the same first name. Maybe that's why it creates such a malevolent vision in my mind.

I look through his charges. He's been in prison for some robberies and assaults, but nothing as bad as I expected. I've taken on clients who are killers. The worst one was a man who killed his own child.

Maybe he won't be as bad as I'm thinking. Not much is worse than a baby murderer. I'm getting myself all worked up for nothing. It wouldn't be the first time I let my anxiety take hold and drive my train of thought.

Then again, maybe the murderers are better than the others. They always come with someone from their parole office, a watchdog to keep everyone safe. Because Maxim isn't a murderer, I'll be alone with him in this little office, completely vulnerable and at the mercy of an ex-convict who isn't deemed dangerous enough to warrant my protection.

I sit down at my computer and search for his name. A few news articles pop up. When I click on the first one, his mugshot fills the screen.

He isn't as intimidating as the figure I conjured in my mind. He's definitely tall at six foot seven, but he isn't as bulky as I expected. Slim but muscular, with broad shoulders that make him look more rugged. Dark hair sits on his head, and it's a mess, though the sides have been neatly shaved. His big green eyes take on a dark cast as he stares at the camera with a smirk.

Judging by this picture, I'm assuming his arrest didn't go all that well. A shiner circles the right eye, and a cut dashes his cheek.

I read the report and see that he attempted to fight off the officers. Yeah, his arrest definitely didn't go well. But it helps to see his face—to get an idea of what to expect before he walks into my office. Before I'm alone with him.

Before I need to try to fix everything that's wrong with him.

Chapter Three

Maxim

I stand by the front door and allow my eyes to ride up the small office building. Dying bushes droop by the door, their curled brown leaves begging for water. It's not very welcoming, even if I *wanted* to go to this appointment. I'd rather do almost anything else than walk in there.

Therapy has never really been my thing. When I first started acting out when I was extremely young, the courts tried to intervene and force me into counseling. I didn't need a therapist to tell me that getting bounced around from one shitty foster home to another had done a number on my psyche.

I was damaged before the foster parents even gave up on me, though. Something has been wrong with me since the day I drew breath. Something not wired quite right.

I pull the door open, and a little electronic alert chimes overhead. A dark-haired young girl sits at the reception desk, playing on her phone, and I'm tempted to leave before she notices me. The prison release papers glue my feet to the floor, though.

"Can I help you?" the girl asks once she looks up from her phone long enough to notice me.

"I'm here for an appointment with Dr. Reeves."

The girl looks at the clock. "You're ten minutes late."

"Sue me," I clip. God, I'm feeling more homicidal by the minute. This girl is lucky I only have eyes for the doctor.

The moment I saw Dr. Reeves' picture, she became my sole focus. I can't stop thinking about her. I dreamed of this visit, but my fantasy took a pretty unethical turn. In my mind, I walked into the office, and she gave me the fuck-me eyes instead of asking me questions. She spread her skirt-clad thighs, and I placed myself between them. Instead of allowing her to force me to confront my demons with her words, I made her confront hers with my dick.

"Have a seat and I'll ask if she's still available to see you," the girl says.

It's ten fucking minutes, not an hour. Did the doctor magically vanish once I didn't appear at the stroke of fucking midnight?

I just nod and pace by the windows lining the wall as I wait.

A few moments later, the girl leads me to a room in the back of the building. The office is nothing like my vision, and neither is the doctor. She can't even be bothered to look up from a manila folder as I enter the room.

"Hello, Mr. Jankowski. Nice of you to finally show up." She closes the manila folder, types something on her laptop, and finally meets my eyes.

Yeah, lady, neither of us wants to be here.

She gestures toward a chair across from her. "Have a seat."

I do, and my jeans rise up as I sit. I drop my head to my fist. There's nothing approachable about my body language, and hers matches mine.

"I'm Dr. Sarah Reeves. I've been a therapist for ten years. Tell me about yourself," she says. When I don't respond, she sighs and starts scribbling something on a yellow legal pad. "It's my understanding that you're here because you're court ordered, correct?"

"Yup."

"Some of my colleagues believe that court-appointed therapy doesn't work. It's a waste of everyone's time. Do you plan to participate?"

It probably is a waste of time, to be honest. "We'll see about that, I guess, huh?"

"Do you have pets or anything, Maxim? Anything you care for?" She swallows as my dark eyes land on her.

"I had a cat, but they took him when I got arrested. I think I need to figure out my own life before I try to take care of something else."

"Fair." She nods. "Have you done therapy before?"

"Nah. Not really my thing."

She leans forward, pushing her breasts higher. I can't keep my eyes away from them, and I don't try.

"But they brought it up to you before?" she asks. "Your parents?"

"My parents tried to bring me to therapy after the loss of my twin," I say coldly.

"How old were you when you lost your brother?"

"It doesn't matter. I don't even remember him."

This is a lie. I remember him. I remember the way he looked when he was up to something, the little quirk of his brow. I remember his laugh. Most of all, I remember the sound of his body colliding with rocks at the bottom of the fucking well.

"What happened to him?"

"He fell down a well on the property."

"How did your parents cope with that loss?"

I sit up. "I don't fucking know. And then they died too, so it doesn't matter."

The air shifts. She no longer looks so sure of herself. Her confidence has drained from her eyes, replaced by a glint of fear.

"Will you tell me more about that?" Her voice quivers a bit, so she clears her throat and sips from a water bottle on her desk.

"Absolutely not," I snap.

She should count herself blessed to have received this much information from me already. I don't need to talk about my brother or my parents. I don't want to. The only other person who knows what happened that day is dead, and I'm done discussing it. She can go look up the article from the fucking paper if she's hungry for more dirty details.

It was all over the news. I was labeled a psychopathic child because I didn't act the way I "should have" after the incident. I saw no point in crying and being miserable. He was already dead. Tormenting myself about it wouldn't bring him back.

"What about your parents?"

"I'm not talking about them." I've had enough. I stand to leave.

"If you exit this room, I'll have to report that you're being non-compliant," she says. She raises her chest, her confidence returning with full force.

I sit down again, look at the clock, and shrug. "Fine. I

guess we'll be silent for the next half hour. Is that compliant enough?"

And that's exactly what we do. We sit in silence as the clock counts the seconds with a monotonous tick that scrapes against the backs of my eyeballs.

I stare at her until her cheeks flush red and she crosses her legs. She grabs her laptop and places it on her lap, then starts typing away. Each clack of the keys unhinges me a little more.

I assume they normally do this shit after the session, but what else can she do during this painful silence between us?

I'm tempted to lean forward and rip the hunk of metal from her hands to read what she's saying about me. I want to see how she's framed what little bit of information I've shared with her when she doesn't even have the full picture.

Go ahead. Micro-analyze and judge me for a few sentences.

I'm used to it. People in my life have thought they understood me, but their misunderstandings are why I'm the way I am today. Why I've done the things I've done.

The clock strikes the hour, and I stand up. I don't look back at her as I whip open the door. "See you next week, doc."

Chapter Four

Sarah

I spin in my chair and twirl a pencil between my fingers. I've been dreading this day since my first tense visit with Maxim last week. I look up at the clock. He's late. Again.

And he's deranged.

My boss doesn't like that word. He wants me to use appropriate terminology, but I just want to call a spade a spade.

Maxim is either psychopathic or sociopathic, but I haven't figured out which one because I've only spent two very guarded hours with him so far. I'm not surprised he went to prison. In fact, I'm more surprised he's *out* of prison. His record wasn't all that lengthy, but his convictions aren't what unnerve me.

When I'm looking at him, I see nerves firing in his mind that are best left dormant. I can almost feel the hum of the devil coming to life when he enters a room. His presence demands my attention, but he doesn't look especially menacing . . . until he speaks. He's—

I turn my chair and see him behind me, leaning against the doorway. Just *watching* me.

Watching me while I think about him.

"Doc," he says as he kicks his foot off the doorway.

"You're late, Maxim. Again."

"I'd come up with a lie, but I'm just really bad at time management, which I hope you can help me with." He takes a seat across from me and folds his large hands in his lap.

He doesn't have issues with time management. He just doesn't give a shit about time—mine *nor* his. I take a deep breath and swivel to face him fully, crossing my legs at my ankles as I bring my laptop closer.

He brushes back dark hair that's faded on the sides, and his chilling green eyes assess me as much as I assess him. His strong arms stretch the sleeves of his shirt as he flexes and tugs a pillow from behind him. He's a piece of fucking art to look at, but this pretty painting is also cursed.

I clear my throat and drop my eyes to the bright screen in front of me. Our last session ended after talking about his childhood. Well, *trying* to talk about his childhood. I had typed **TRAUMATIZED** in big bold letters, underlined and everything, regarding something he experienced as a child. He gave me very little information, but researching the news articles from the incident gave me more. It unfolded much differently than his brother just "falling into a well."

His twin brother had gone missing, and he watched their mother mourn for weeks. Maxim had witnessed his brother's death, yet he said *nothing* to anyone. Even as police and searchers scoured the land for the missing child, even as his mother wept in her bed, he remained absolutely stone cold about it.

Who the fuck just . . . keeps quiet about where the body is? What happened to him?

I'm assuming the event caused serious damage to his psyche, whether he wants to admit it or not. Or was he like that before the incident? We'll likely never know because his parents died in a fire a few years after his brother's death. Maxim was the sole survivor, escaping with only second-degree burns on his forearms. Webbed scarring marks the event on his skin.

Suspicion forms in my mind, though I try to fight it off. As a psychiatrist, it's not my place to fabricate fiction about my clients. But I can't shake the unsettling feeling in my stomach. His presence is enough to make me uncomfortable, but the more I uncover about his past, the more I want to bury it again. I don't want to learn more.

But I have to. It's my job.

I scroll down the page. "We touched base on your childhood last time, Maxim. What about your teenage years? Did you go to high school or anything?"

He leans back and interlaces his fingers behind his head. His shirt rides up his muscled abdomen. "So we're back to this?"

"Yes, Maxim. We have to try to talk about . . . something." Anything. I'm not particular.

He scoffs. "I did, for a year. I got through tenth grade and dropped out after my foster mother died in a tragic car accident. It's too hard for me to talk about her death," he says, as cold and stone-faced as ever. It doesn't take my doctorate to know that he's faking emotions, and poorly at that.

Death follows him. A path of bodies in his past. Maybe in his wake.

I turn to my computer and begin typing.

```
Maxim is very affectless regarding
the death of his foster mother. He
couldn't be more despondent. Socio-
pathic tendencies?
```

"What happened to you once your foster mother died?" I ask.

"Juvie. Then jail. And now I'm in your office, doc," he says with a shrug.

I'd like to know more about that section of his past, but juvie records would be sealed, and I doubt he'll be honest if I ask. I try anyway. "What were you in juvenile detention for?"

He throws me another shrug. "Assault."

His violent history. The deaths. I brush my hand over the back of my neck to try to pat down the raised hairs. Though I try to stop my mind from formulating an opinion, my heart knows the truth: He isn't innocent. He's the catalyst for every loss he's experienced. It's not there in black-and-white, but it's there in a very damning shade of gray.

"Care to elaborate on this assault?"

"Nah, I'm good, doc." He goes silent.

"So we're back to this?" I throw his words back at him.

He replies with a sinful smirk, his eyes darkening as they settle on mine.

The clock on the wall ticks away the time, the sound growing until it thunders in my ears. Then, sudden realization hits me. I'm in a dark and desolate office, alone with him. If he wants to repeat the behaviors from his past, I'd be helpless to it. I have expired pepper spray in my purse, but I'd be dead before I could even find the damn thing. He could do anything he wanted to me.

Anything.

I make a mental note to move his future appointments to a time when office staff is still around. But even then, with staff present, could they really protect me from someone like him?

Chapter Five

Maxim

"Back to what, doc?"

She stares at the smirk on my face, knowing damn well we aren't "back to" anything. Walking through that door doesn't change who I am at my core. No matter how pretty she is, she can't break through the barrier I built to keep everyone out. She can't make me spill my feelings, and she can't fix the fuckery in my mind.

If she continues to press me, she'll regret it once she hears what comes out of my mouth. I already see how she looks at me. Like she can view the evil in my heart. Joke's on her. I have no heart. But I do have a brain, and that organ is mildly *obsessed* with her.

I like how she dresses. Tight black skirts that go to her knees. Black stockings that conceal her pale legs and give an air of professionalism to her outfit. Silk dress shirts peek from beneath suit jackets. She always dresses the same. She keeps a pair of bright running shoes by her desk, though.

Probably to wear on her commute home instead of her dark heels.

When I walked in, I saw her twisting her pencil around her long fingers, dreading our appointment as much as I anticipated it. I managed to talk my dick down before she noticed, but the surprised dread on her face almost made me hard all over again. There's something sexy about forcing my presence on a woman like her. Making her sit in a room with me while she squirms because she'd rather be anywhere else.

Yeah, I like that shit.

I remember the feeling I got when I looked her up online. Dr. Sarah Reeves, alumna of a prestigious college, with ten years under her belt in her own practice. In her picture, she looked so different. So prim and proper, with her dark hair parted to the side, a fake smile plastered on her face, and big brown eyes that said, *I'll analyze the fuck out of you.* I liked it. I couldn't wait to see her in person.

So I didn't.

I followed her to and from the office for about a week before our appointment. By the time I met her, I felt like I already knew her.

She'll never know me, though. Not more than what I let her learn. While Sarah tries to pry into my mind, my mind pries into *her*. It splits her body open with my thoughts. As she asks her questions, I make sure I give her enough of me to keep her engaged so I can keep fucking her in my mind, taking her on every surface in this office.

In my fantasy, she loves it, but in reality, she'd hate me *and* herself.

"I think that's it for today," Sarah says, a non-subtle hint of annoyance in her tone. Her distaste for me is clear. Even the way she crosses her legs showcases her disgust.

I offer her a sick, twisted smirk that pisses her off worse. "See you later, doc," I say, leaning close to her as I get up.

She clutches her jacket and pulls it tighter, fully covering herself. I drink up her unease. My mere existence terrifies her. Imagine if I opened my underbelly and showed her the dark, diseased insides. I'd cover her in my blood, ruin all that beautiful, perfect skin with my tainted crimson.

Then I'd spread her legs and break her.

Ruin her.

And she'd thank me for destroying her before taking my dick again. Because that's what's brewing in her fucked-up little mind.

She doesn't know it yet, but she'd love to be fucked by someone she can't fix. To be treated like a whore by someone she can't reach would drive her nuts, and she'd take it out on my dick. She'd fuck me harder because I'm emotionally guarded. Psychologically damaged.

Fuck, a guy can dream, can't he?

I leave the building and head to the beater car I was able to borrow off one of the losers at the house. He doesn't go anywhere anyway, so I may buy it off him when I get a little extra cash.

Her gaze follows me from her office window as I walk across the parking lot. I feel her stare burning through my shirt. When I turn to face her, she zips the blinds closed. She couldn't want me less, and that only makes me want her more.

I froth over her like a rabid fucking dog salivating with obsessive need. If only she knew what she does to me. How her disgust drives me wild with madness I'm already running from.

I sit in the car and take a deep breath before unzipping my jeans and wrapping my hand around my cock. I can't even wait until I get home to touch myself to thoughts of her.

My hand strokes my length, and I squeeze my balls to give myself the pain I need to come. I wouldn't need to hurt myself to get off if I could just fuck her right now. She's a bitter little vessel for me to dump my load inside, and I'd only need her mouth or her cunt.

But she's not here. She's hiding in her office.

I hope curiosity gets the better of her and she looks out to see me furiously jerking off to her. That would make for an interesting next session. The tempo of my hand increases as I think about teaching the doc a little something about me as I fuck her senseless.

Maybe I'll whisper in her ear, tell her I'm a deranged killer as I empty my balls inside her. Her whimpers of pleasure will be replaced by screams of horror as I drip down her creamy thighs. By the time those words leave my lips, it'll be too late. She'd struggle to fall asleep that night while remembering how she came on a killer's dick, and despite what she feels, the realization that she'd do it again.

I spill my come to the thoughts of her. Pearly white pours down my hand, rolling over my skin. I smirk, get out of my car, sneak across the lot, and wipe my gift on the office doorknob. I hope she touches it when she locks up tonight. I hope her fingers glide through the sticky white substance.

Maybe she'll be too stressed and overworked to even take more than a second to notice before she wipes it on her tight little skirt. She's certainly too proud to ask me if I left the gift at our next session.

Either way, I hope she drives to her nice home with my come staining her skin.

Unethical

I wipe the residue off on my jeans and stare at the door to the building. "Next week, doc."

Chapter Six

Sarah

I stand by the big office window. The blinds are firmly closed, but a crease runs through one of the plastic pieces, creating a gap between the slats. My eyes narrow as his car pulls out of the parking lot.

An eerie chill rakes my arms, and goosebumps rise over my skin as I recall what I just witnessed. He'd stared at the closed blinds covering my window, and just the memory of his heavy gaze makes my cheeks flush with heat. It was as if he could see me through the dark blinds. Then he'd looked straight ahead before dropping his head back.

Even though I didn't want to admit it at the time, I knew what he was doing. And I wasn't surprised. God, he's such a creep.

So why did I find myself sticking a finger between the slats and widening it just a little?

I couldn't see any details behind the dark windows, but the movement was enough to paint a picture. I'm nauseated by the thought of him touching himself to me. And it's not a far stretch to say that's what he was thinking of while he pleasured himself. I see how he stares at me when he's here, with a hunger that leaves me feeling naked and dirty.

But maybe I'm imagining it. Maybe I've imagined all of this. Instead of yanking on his dick and throwing his head back in the heat of the moment, maybe he was just scratching a really pesky itch on his foot.

Then I remember how his dark eyes had landed on the window again, and I'd ripped my fingers away and thrown myself against the wall. I try to calm my breathing as this memory overtakes my senses.

I hate him.

I hate our sessions.

This is a complete waste of time.

He doesn't want to be here, and I don't want to be within five feet of him. Or one hundred feet, considering what I just witnessed in the parking lot. But there's something about him that stupidly makes me want to cut him open and let his insides spill all over me. I want to pull him apart and understand how someone becomes so fucked up and disconnected from reality and other human beings.

Doesn't he want to connect with someone? Aren't we all born with that innate desire to be someone's something? A friend. A lover. Shit, even an enemy.

He doesn't even seem like the type to have an enemy. That would require emotion, which is something I'm sure he's incapable of. If he killed his brother, it wasn't an act perpetrated out of hatred. It was probably a gut reaction to some morbid curiosity flitting around in his brain. For someone like Maxim, his brother would have been a thing, not a person. It would be no different than seeing how a broom fairs when shoved inside a woodchipper.

Fuck, why am I comparing a dead little boy to a broom?

I drop my head into my hand and rub the small stretch of skin between my eyebrows. Is mental illness contagious? Can my patients' long list of personality disorders rub off on me?

I think they become a part of me, in some way. The more sessions I have with my multitude of patients, the more I begin to question my dwindling sanity. Even sessions with people like Maxim, when our time together is absolutely dreadful and unproductive, begin to seep into me. It's like he's crawled inside me to live in my mind.

Or infect it.

I guess that's what happens when my one job is to get inside their heads. It's hard to do that without letting them into mine too. But how else can I learn how they tick? Trust must be built. A delicate push and pull must be performed. I let them in a little, they let me in a little, and then I get all the dirty little details they're too scared to share at first.

But that's not what I want to do with him. Maxim is too ill to become a part of me. Too deranged to let inside my heart. Something about him leaves me with this nagging certainty that he's worse than any of the other patients I've worked with. So much pain and suffering reside in my soul because of the men and women before him, and I don't think I can take on any more of it.

I drop into my leather chair with a sigh and pull my laptop closer. As I bring up the internet browser, the search bar glares at me. I fight the urge, but I eventually give in and type his name into that little white rectangle. The same news stories and mugshots fill my screen.

Does he have to be so ruggedly handsome?

I groan and drop my head to the desk. I shouldn't think about a patient this way, but especially not a patient as dangerous as Maxim. A violent offender. And though it hasn't been proven, probably a child murderer. I only have one course of action now.

With a shaking hand, I pick up the phone and call his probation officer.

As the phone rings, I wonder if I'm doing the right thing. I want to help him, I truly do, but I don't want to lose myself in the process. There are only so many pieces of my soul left.

A voice comes across the line, and I nearly jump out of my skin. I clear my throat. "Hey, Frank. It's Sarah, Sarah Reeves, Maxim Jankowski's therapist."

"What's the matter, Sarah? Is he behaving himself?"

No.

Yes.

He hasn't done anything . . . yet. It's the future actions of Maxim Jankowski I worry about most. But I'd sound crazy if I said that.

"Yes, he's fine. The problem is, I just don't think I'm the right fit for him."

"Ms. Reeves, the other therapists have overburdened caseloads. You're the only one in our program who has any availability. If you can't provide the court-ordered course of therapy, we have no choice but to take him back into custody and allow the prison shrinks to take a crack at him. Is that what you think he needs?"

Gaslighting prick. I don't want to be the reason he's sent back to prison, but if something happens to me, this is on them.

"No." I take a breath. "I'll figure it out."

Frank tries to release a sigh of relief as quietly as he can, but it still blows like a gale-force wind into the receiver on his end. "Take care of yourself."

Unethical

What a fucking ominous farewell. And it doesn't make me feel any better about my sacrificial decision to keep him out of prison. I sure hope I don't end up regretting this.

Chapter Seven

Maxim

Sarah's shoulders drop the moment she locks the office door, as if the weight of her clients' lives presses her down. Her eyes show that same heaviness. She doesn't look up from the ground as she walks toward her car.

She's been working past nine every night since our session four days ago. Like a well-trained dog, she repeats her routine again tonight. She gets inside her fancy little BMW and pulls out of her reserved parking spot. The placard with her name on it made it exceptionally easy to figure out which car belonged to her. Not a good safeguard from people like me who are predisposed to obsession and subsequent stalking.

I turn on the engine and follow her. Not too close, though. I don't know if she'll recognize my car or if she's in too much of a haze to do so, and I don't want to take any chances. I tail her to her home, though I already know the way and could follow the route in my sleep at this point.

When she nears her driveway, I hang back and park a little ways down the dark suburban street. Then I walk toward her house, hiding among the trees that decorate either side of the unlit street as I near my destination.

Her house sits further from the road than the others. Tucked away in the woods at the end of the dead-end street, it's the perfect setting for what I plan to do. How fortunate for me.

How unfortunate for her.

I take my place behind the drooping oak tree so I can watch her. Sarah does the same thing every night when she comes home. Her quirks are so fucking cute. She waits in her car for one to three minutes as she finishes the song on the radio. When she gets out, she checks her car handle three times, then tucks her purse beneath her right arm before she unlocks her front door. She's regimented.

But now, so am I. This is what I do every night.

I watch her.

It's become a necessity. Just as necessary as the stringent rules outlined on my paperwork from prison.

Go to therapy? Check.

Become obsessed with every breath my therapist takes? Check.

Obsessively watch her from the fucking bushes? Check.

Imagine how afraid she'd be if she saw me? How tormented she'd feel? Check and check.

Sarah enters the house and turns on the living room light, illuminating her form as she passes the window. She sheds her suit jacket and hangs it up. It's the only time I get to see the lacy undershirt that I think about during our sessions. Her breasts draw the fabric down, bunching it beneath their full curves.

Fuck, I want to rip those buttons off with my teeth. I

want to take those clothes off her body and devour her. Hopefully, she tells me no. To stop. Because that would be delicious.

I stroke the front of my jeans, anticipating my favorite part of my nightly routine. The heat of excitement courses through my veins as it maps its way to my dick. I ache for her. She keeps me hard, even when I'm away from her, but nothing makes me throb like seeing her through the window. Invading her personal space. Pleasing myself to her blissful ignorance.

The upstairs bathroom faces the woods. The seclusion gives her the confidence to leave her curtains open. The light turns on, and I snap my attention to it. She comes into view and strips off her shirt, slowly, almost as if she knows I'm watching her. Like she's putting on a show for me. But I know that's not true.

She would freak out if she saw me, not put on a show. She'd clutch that shirt to her body to hide what I'm so desperate to see.

Her breasts relax as she unfastens the back clasp on her bra. Her tits squeeze together again as she tugs down each strap. After she removes her bra, she drops her hands to her skirt. The stiff material glides past her ass and slips down her thighs. I imagine how the fabric might feel in my hands as I unzip my jeans and pull my cock from the slit.

I have wanted little more than to have my hands on her. I don't even care in what form. I don't even care if she's awake to feel my touch.

She gets in the shower and closes the door. I see only the pixelated outline of her body through the glass. I lean back against the tree and stroke myself. My imagination runs wild.

I imagine sitting on the flimsy couch in her office, my

thighs spread and her head bobbing on my dick as she sucks it. I imagine choking her with my cock. I'd call her doc, mock her weakness for fucking a client, and impale her throat afterward. I envision the drool all over her pretty chin as she sucks me off.

She comes out of the shower with her hair slick against her neck. As she reaches for a towel, her big, beautiful tits pull together before spreading again as she dries herself off.

She hasn't smiled once since leaving the office. It's kind of sad. The woman needs to be dicked down, but she'd never let me be the one to do it.

Sarah looks out the window. I sink against the base of the tree, even though I'm *pretty* sure she can't see me, but I'm not positive she can't. That's what I love about jerking off out here. The risk of getting caught by her. The anger and fear on her face would be so worth it, even though I know her fear would precede lights and sirens and a return trip to prison.

Honestly, I won't mind returning to prison if I can go back with my mind full of her and my balls empty. And that's a dangerous thought.

Chapter Eight

Sarah

I get in the shower after another long day of sessions. Steam engulfs me, and I breathe it in through my nose and out through my mouth, just like I teach my overly anxious patients. Behind closed doors, I'm one of them. I'm just as anxious and unsure. Just as nervous about the monster hiding under the bed.

The breathing exercise works, and soon I'm centered once more. It's been a trying day. With certain patients, the hour flies by and I enjoy the productivity of our conversations. With others, the hour drags and we get nowhere. I'm forced to sift through the different methods we learned in school to draw a useful sentence out of them. Today was more of the latter, and it's been exhausting.

Maxim's sessions are like that. I find the end of a string and pull, but there's no give from his side. I sigh as I remember that I have to meet with him tomorrow. It's been a week already? How?

My gaze drifts to the gap at the edge of the shower

curtain, and I peer into the darkness beyond the window. Sometimes I feel watched, as if I'm not alone in my own home. But I am. In fact, I haven't had someone in my house in a long time.

I'm a workaholic, which means I don't have much time for relationships. Hell, I hardly make time for myself. At the end of the day, I barely have the energy to stand in the shower or brush my teeth, let alone something as frivolous as reading, painting my nails, or indulging in a hobby. Self-care isn't in my vocabulary.

How strange that I don't take the time to find my happiness, yet I'm expected to help others find theirs.

I've considered getting a pet to break up the monotony. It might not be so bad to come home and vent my frustrations to another living being, especially when that living being can't speak back. Then I think of all the care an animal requires, and I'm just not up for that right now. I can barely take care of my own needs.

I'm tired of carrying my clients' problems and horrific pasts like a weight around my neck. No one should be expected to cart around their own baggage along with everyone else's. They don't teach you how to deal with these things in school—the burnout and fatigue.

The mental illnesses you inherit.

Warm water washes away today's efforts. I drop my head to the wall, letting the spray focus on the back of my neck, where my tension is carried. I want to call out tomorrow. It's my damn business, and I should be able to take a mental-health day. I'm allowed to be weak sometimes.

But then I remember my client tomorrow. I'm under pressure because of Maxim's mandated status, which makes me feel mandated, too. I groan. I'll never make any progress with him. Instead of speaking the truth, he just vomits some convoluted version of events, and I can't help him if he can't be honest with me. Or himself.

Worst of all, his presence sucks the air out of the room, leaving me in a silent void that slowly suffocates me. I've never met a human more capable of applying pressure with a mere look.

I think about how he watched me through the blinds of my office, peering through me in a way no one ever has.

My hand rides down my body and hangs up on every imperfection that I become acutely aware of. What does he see when he looks at me? The slight weight gain? The bags under my eyes? Or something more?

I imagine someone touching me. Not Maxim, though. Anyone but him. I dip my hand between my legs and run my fingertips along the fine hairs that cover my mound. My touch pries apart my lips, and I circle my fingers until it starts to feel good.

I lean against the shower wall and arch my back as I drag the showerhead lower. The spray of water works my body, and I pretend strong, manly hands grip my hips as some stranger drops to his knees and licks me.

My eyes close, and I tilt my pelvis as moans grip my throat. When I imagine the hands on me, I realize I'm not envisioning a stranger. Those are Maxim's hands. I recognize the artwork that runs up his forearms.

I open my eyes, rip the showerhead away, and slam my hand against the wall. Goddamn it. I just wanted to enjoy one thing. One. I want to forget about my job for a minute so I can get off and release the tension that ripples beneath every inch of my skin.

So why am I thinking about him?

There's a draw to learn more about him, even though I know I won't like what I discover. When I peel back the layers of others, I usually find a soft inner core that needs nurturing. No matter how I peel Maxim, what lies beneath will surely be hard and toxic. Dangerous. I'm inclined to leave his layers untouched and make it through this mandated course of therapy as best I can. But it doesn't help that he's infiltrating my thoughts and interrupting my life by existing in the same fucking world as me.

I get out of the shower, grab my towel, and rub it through my hair. When I drag the brush through the wet strands, I leave too much hair behind. It's the stress. The eating takeout almost every night. The long hours spent at a desk. It's not giving myself grace.

I wrap the towel around my waist and wipe the fog from the mirror. I lift my shoulder and smile, remembering the lesson I was taught to tell others: Smiling at yourself can release the feel-good hormones we need to be happy.

So does getting yourself off, but that isn't happening for me now. So I smile at myself like a fucking idiot, as if a facial expression can fix all of this.

And like a big, shitty cherry on top, I have to meet with Maxim tomorrow. I have to wear this smile and sit in front of him while he analyzes me as much as I try to analyze him.

There's a darkness in him that I don't want to shed light on. It's safer for me to leave him in the shadows.

But it's my job to hold a flashlight inside these dark spaces. To look around until something skitters from the recesses and steps into the beam of truth. What hides within Maxim is more likely to charge forward instead of skittering, though, and instead of stepping toward truth, I have a sinking feeling it will go straight for my throat.

I'll need to be more cautious moving forward.

Chapter Nine

Maxim

"Have you been able to hold a job?" she asks.

What a stupid question. Of course not. People don't readily jump at the chance to hire a felon.

"Nah, but I'm currently working under the table for a mechanic. Learned quite a bit about cars while on the inside."

She starts talking about how a routine would be good for me. I hardly listen. I'm too busy staring at the silky deep-green shirt beneath the buttons of her jacket.

Since I started watching her, her breasts have become familiar to me, and I focus on the bare image of them in my mind. I can see them so perfectly, and it makes me hard as fuck. I cross my legs to keep her from noticing. I imagine ripping off her jacket, then that silky shirt and black bra, and devouring her chest as I raise the front of her skirt.

"Maxim? Are you listening to me?" she asks, a sharp rise in her tone.

No, I'm not listening, because I'm imagining her mouth being used for something besides analyzing me. I'm thinking about her last night.

I'm pretty certain she was using that showerhead for nefarious purposes. I wonder what she was thinking about. Was it one of her many clients? Could it have been me? Have I wormed my way into her mind yet?

"Yes, doc. Routine is vital to my rehabilitation, yadda, yadda."

She crosses her arms over her chest. "Do you even want to be helped?"

No. But I can't say that. Like a fish on the end of a line, I need to string her along at least a little bit. "Of course I do."

"Then why are you so closed off about your past? Your present? What am I supposed to talk to you about?"

I'd prefer it if she used that mouth for something other than analyzing me, but here we are. She breaks her professional facade and allows her shoulders to fall. She sighs.

I'm frustrating her, and I love it.

"I do my best, doc. I wasn't raised to talk about my feelings. It's not gonna happen overnight." I reel out a little more line, a sentence that makes her think she's peeled back a thin layer to learn more about me. She hasn't, but I'm happy to let her think she has.

Her shoulders rise, as if my words have rejuvenated her. It's so cute. "Tell me how you were raised, Maxim."

"I mostly raised myself." I smirk because I've only pretended to open the door so I could close it in her face once more. I've gone right back to dead-end answers.

She blows out a breath and clicks her pen once. "I'm done with this session. I'm clearly the only one taking our sessions seriously, and I can't help you if you don't want to help yourself. You're welcome to stay for the hour, but I'm done placating you today."

She stands up, goes to her desk, and plops down in the cushiony computer chair. From the top left drawer, she produces a pair of reading glasses. She slides them over the slender bridge of her nose and proceeds to ignore the fuck out of me.

It's hot.

I like how she looks with her glasses on. So prim and proper. So different from the man sitting across the room from her.

I want to ruin her. Steal every ounce of innocence from her body and fill her with my evilness. Corrupt her with my depravity. Make her forget all about wanting to selflessly help people and teach her to focus on selfishly getting the attention she so desperately craves.

I consider whipping out my dick and jerking off to her right here, but then she'll end our sessions for good. I can't have that. I want more time with her, not less.

There must be some way to get her to let *her* walls down, and I'm pretty sure I know just what would do it. That woman needs to be fucked and filled. Pleased and teased. I want her to forget everything she's ever learned except my name. I need her to crave the man she despises.

I might even let her inside if she let me inside her first. That seems like a fair trade.

I stand up, and she tenses. I make my way across her office, and she tightens her grip on the mouse to keep her hand from trembling. It doesn't work. The jitter in her muscles might be slight, but like a hawk viewing a mouse in the grass, I see every twitch of movement.

"What're writing about me, doc?" I lean down to look at the screen, but she turns it toward the window with a scowl.

"None of your business," she says.

"If it's about me, doesn't that make it my business?"

A lock of hair lies across her neck, so I lean closer and blow it away from the gentle thud of her pulse. She shoves her hand against her throat to shield her precious skin from my warm breath, but I don't miss the goosebumps rising from her flesh. I affect her, even if she won't admit it.

"Fine, don't get yourself all worked up," I say. "I was just curious."

I stand up straight and wipe my hands down my jeans, smoothing my lap. Her eyes stay glued to the screen, but if she just turns a fraction of an inch toward me, she'll get an eyeful of my dick straining against the fabric.

Would she scream if she noticed how hard I am for her? I'm certain she would, but I'm less certain of the emotion behind that sound. Disgust, no doubt, but would she be disgusted with me, or with herself for liking what she sees?

"I'll see you next week," I say. "Who knows, I might even be more willing to talk by then."

"Doubt it," she says under her breath.

She needs to watch that pretty mouth of hers. If she keeps it up, I might not be able to control myself. I love her snark too much. It contradicts the face—the *facade*—she shows everyone else.

Everyone but me.

She's not the sweet professional she wants everyone else to believe. I see the real Sarah Reeves. And she's mine.

Chapter Ten

Sarah

My next patient comes in soon after Maxim leaves. Her dress sleeve hangs off her shoulder, and she looks as manic as she always does. She plops down with an exaggerated sigh, tugs up her sleeve, and begins her sordid tale where we left off last time.

I don't even need to speak, but I interrupt her to force out my cursory introduction. There aren't enough hours in the day to get to the bottom of what's wrong with Mrs. Birch.

Newly and unhappily married. Pregnant again, with a one-year-old at home who runs her ragged. She told me this baby was an attempt to save her marriage. The non-professional in me wanted to ask if that has ever worked in the history of marriages. From my many years in this very chair, I can attest that it has not.

I don't have kids myself. My biological clock is ticking away, and the way she talks about being a mother makes me glad I'm running out of time. I realize how terrible this must sound, but then again, I've never been in a relationship long enough to *want* to have children.

Maybe my viewpoint would be a little different if I'd been with someone that screamed "daddy material," but most of the men I've dated have been poster children for people who need therapy, and I'm not the person who can psycho-support a partner. I'd rather stay single and childless than have a baby and be forced to care for the baby *and* the other parent.

I think all of these things as Mrs. Birch drones on in the background. My focus has entirely flown the proverbial coop. But how can I focus on any patients after I've had a session with Maxim?

My chest is a permanent shade of red from the frustration he drums up inside me. He's playing a cruel game by relaying snippets of information about his life without ever giving me the full story. He pretends to nibble the bait at the end of the hook, but he's only looping it around detritus at the bottom of the pond. I'm perpetually snagged, and I need to cut the line and let him loose. Half the stuff that comes out of his mouth is probably a lie anyway.

Mrs. Birch blabbers on in the background as she picks at her nails and fiddles with the collar on her haggard dress. She talks about everything that's ever happened in her life, and I should really listen to what she has to say. But I can't. My thoughts continue to circle Maxim.

The way he stood over me.

The way his breath felt as he blew on my neck.

He's equally terrifying and intriguing, and something about him makes me want to break through to him even though it's so fucking stupid to want to get anywhere near him. To even let him get close to me again would be suicidal. For my safety and sanity, I should avoid Maxim at all costs.

There's only one problem. I can't.

I get paid to subject myself to him. Sitting across from him pays my fucking bills. And that means I'm stuck in this unrelenting situation for a little while longer.

I look out the window, and the hair on the back of my neck stands on end. I can't shake the feeling that I'm being watched.

While nodding and pretending to listen to the woman in front of me, I scan the cars in the parking lot. Even though I don't see his vehicle, I still can't seem to break free from the mounting anxiety and the feeling that he's out there.

Mrs. Birch has moved on in her monologue. As she talks about her dreams—something about being chased by a giant turkey who can speak—I squint through the blinds to see if anyone is in fact watching me. Even if Maxim's car isn't out there, he could still be lurking in the shadows.

That's the most annoying thing about Maxim. He forces his way into my thoughts, no matter where I am. At work. At home. In the grocery store. He's the boogeyman lurking in the shadows, ready to pounce on me.

He's not, obviously. Not really. But he continues to infiltrate my mental barriers. He continues to cause a rising tide of anxiety that will drown me if I'm not careful. He's created a riptide, and I'm standing in the danger zone.

"Dr. Reeves, are you listening to me?" Mrs. Birch asks, her soft voice rising to an annoyed snip.

A bit of heat rushes into my cheeks. This woman pays me good money to listen to her, but I'm too busy working through my own issues to focus on hers. What a great shrink I am.

"Yes," I say. "I'm just going to close these blinds real quick."

I stand up and walk toward the big window overlooking the parking lot. Now that I have a clearer view, my eyes scan the entire lot again to see if I see anything or anyone out of place.

My car is a hair's width from hitting the pole in front of it, but that's the only thing of note I see. There's no sign of him.

Maxim is gone. Thank god.

With a silent sigh of relief, I pull down on the string beside the blinds, and the plastic planks slam closed. A renewed darkness hangs over us, so I flip on the overhead light.

"You were telling me about that dream you keep having," I say before sitting down again. "The one about the turkey?"

At least, I hope that's what she was talking about. I admit, I did start to space. It's easy to do with talkative clients. I'm very much grounded when I'm in the sessions with Maxim, fighting and trying to pry every syllable of information out of him until, frankly, I'm exhausted.

Goddamn it, there I go again. I wish he'd stop occupying my thoughts. I wish he'd leave me the fuck alone in my mind. I'll be glad when we have our last session and I never have to come face to face with that man again.

Chapter Eleven

Maxim

My boots squeak on linoleum floors within the grocery store. I'm not lifting my feet enough. I haven't had the opportunity to see the doctor in one of my private "sessions" today, so maybe I'm feeling a little fucking lost without her.

As if the devil smiles up at me, I turn the corner at the end of the bread aisle and see her. My shoes squeal more from the abrupt stop, and I leap backward to keep her from spotting me. Peering past the corner, I watch her lift and fondle various cantaloupes. Her dainty fingers squeeze and palpate the textured rind, and my cock hardens at the sight of each movement. I wish she would touch me with half the focus.

I wish she'd touch me at all.

My breathing quickens. I can almost smell her from here—the mild perfume barely overpowering the fruity body wash she would have bathed in.

Sarah puts the large cantaloupe aside, grabs the one beneath it, puts it into the cart, and hurries off. She seems to be in a perpetual rush, as if she doesn't have time to do anything other than work.

I consider following her, but I can't stop thinking about her hands on that cantaloupe. She touched it with such focus before she discarded it. My predetermined steps lead me toward the island of fruit before I even realize my compulsion. An older woman waddles over to the same spot, and her hand moves toward the cantaloupe the doc handled.

"If you touch that melon, I will follow you home and kill you," I say.

She clutches her chest, and I take the opportunity to grab my fruit. She's too shocked to speak as I put it under my arm and head toward the checkout.

I rush through a purchase that's become a hyper-focus in my mind. I can't stop thinking about the way Sarah's delicate fingers moved over the little pits in the outer skin. I keep my hand on my little prize as I hurry to my car and drive to the halfway house.

No one questions me as I carry it beneath my arm and head inside. Just a friendly nod from a neighbor as I walk by. I probably look like I'm on a health kick, finally getting my life on track. Or they think I'm half nutty with a fruit friend. Either way, I don't give a fuck. Caring about the thoughts of others hasn't stopped me before, and it won't stop me now.

I bring the cantaloupe to my bed, take my knife from beneath the mattress, and stab the blade through the thick rind. I dig and spin and cut until I've crafted a perfect hole. My dick twitches as my fingers graze the same ridges that felt the doctor's grazing touch. I reach down, unzip my pants, and free myself.

With a bite of my lip, I lean back and turn the fruit over, lowering the hole onto my cock. The orange flesh strains around my girth. I moan and touch the melon's rough exterior as if I'm feeling her as I fuck myself with her body.

"Fuck, doc," I groan as the meat of the fruit squelches and moves away from the intrusion.

I fuck myself harder and faster, and juice drips onto the front of my pants. I catch some in my hand and bring it to my mouth. My fingers slip past my lips as I imagine the sweetness is hers.

Using my other hand, I continue to fuck myself with the fruit. It takes my whole palm to guide it. My muscles flex and tighten as I feel like I'm about to push through the rind on the other side. This is how hard I'd fuck her if I had her in front of me. How I'd tear her in two if I had the opportunity.

No, not if.

When.

There's only so much more control I have left when even the sight of her fingers on a hunk of fruit makes me need to fuck it.

I grip the cantaloupe with both hands and slow my thrusts. My body heat has warmed the soft flesh inside. If I close my eyes, I can almost imagine it's something human. I can pretend it's her pretty little pussy as I come inside it.

And just like that, the thought of filling her sends a bolt of pleasure riding up my spine. A thick groan leaves my lips as I unload, spreading creamy white within the orange flesh.

I pull my cock from the fruit, and my skin gleams with the warm wetness. I lift the cantaloupe, turn it upside down, and hold it over my waiting mouth. Beads of come drip onto my tongue, with a soft, sweet, fruity flavor following it.

"Soon, doc. Soon you'll be the one filled, and not this fucking fruit."

This isn't an empty threat. It's a promise, and I plan to keep it.

Chapter Twelve

Sarah

He's late again, by almost thirty minutes this time. I scheduled this appointment at the end of my day so that his presence doesn't interfere with my time with the clients who are unfortunate enough to come in after him. Now? Now I'm about three seconds away from closing up and documenting him as delinquent.

I tap my pen on the computer desk, giving him exactly five more minutes to come to his *mandatory* appointment. The bitterness inside me subsides as I stare at the screen. Maxim is an ex-con. He could have gotten into a fight with someone at the halfway house. He could have overdosed on an illegal substance. Hell, he could be dead for all I know.

Should I call the police instead of his probation officer? Should I have them do a welfare check instead of sending him back to prison?

I stop flicking the pen on the table. If he were in fact dead, that would be a blessing for me. So why does it *almost* bother me when I realize that I may never see him again?

I think it's because I haven't gotten through to him yet. Maybe it's a fear that I was unable to help him. But I also fear there's something more I'm rationalizing away.

"Hey, doc," he says from the doorway.

I didn't even hear him come in. I probably looked like I was off in la-la land, which I was. Thinking about his demise, mostly.

"Maxim, you're . . ." I look at the clock. I've spent ten minutes lost in my thoughts. "Forty minutes late."

"I had car problems," he says. His calm demeanor irritates me to no end.

"You have my work phone number. You could have called to let me know you were running behind."

He shrugs, sits on the couch, and crosses one leg over his thigh. A Tupperware container rests on his lap.

"What's that?" I ask.

"This?" He lifts it off his lap, and something pale and orange rattles inside. He pulls off the lid and displays the cut-up pieces of fruit. "It's cantaloupe. I brought some for you. It's one of my favorites."

Mine too.

I force a smile as I take it from him, but it's not an entirely fake smile. This small act seems nice of him. Almost as if he's changed his stripes. But I don't know how I feel about this random act of kindness. It doesn't seem in his nature. It seems entirely unnatural for him to be anything but threatening and mysterious.

I set the container on the desk with no intention of doing anything but tossing it into the trash once he leaves. Even if this is a genuine act of kindness on his part, my lack of trust won't allow me to take a risk. Considering the fact that everyone close to him has ended up dead, a few bites of cantaloupe aren't worth my life.

Plus, I'm still upset with him for being late.

"Thank you, Maxim, but you can't just stroll in here with twenty minutes left and expect this session to count."

"Can you give me a break, doc? Have you seen the beater I'm forced to drive? I'm lucky I got here at all."

"I'm not trying to give you a hard time, but the courts—"

"Disrespectfully, fuck the courts. You can put that I was here for a whole day if you wanted to. You could tell them I *lived* at this office if you felt compelled to do so. You can say anything you want to the courts, which means you can say I was here since five o'clock. Right?"

My lips tighten. "You're asking me to lie on your paperwork?"

"Yes," he says, shamelessly.

Maxim stands up and towers over me. He puts his hands on my chair's armrests as he leans closer. Each exhale that rushes out of him brushes the hair from my neck. He's that close. I focus on my breathing to keep from showing any fear.

He smirks at me. "Come on, doc."

He's trying to intimidate me, and it works. It fucking works.

"Fine, Maxim, but just this once."

"Bad, bad doctor," he says.

The way I focus on how his mouth moves is criminal. Just like what I'm doing to his fucking record. But I have an ulterior motive.

"But only on one condition," I add. "At our next session, you have to open up."

He shrugs, and I take that as an agreement.

"Since I'm already fudging my records for you, we should pick this up next week." I lift my chin. "On time."

"Yes ma'am. See you next week."

He takes his hands off my chair and rights himself. His finger taps on the top of the Tupperware. "Can I get this back when you're done with it?"

"Of course."

"Enjoy," he says as he strides toward the door and leaves.

A stale silence permeates the room once his footsteps recede down the hall. My eyes catch on the container's red lid as my growling stomach disrupts the quiet. I really shouldn't have skipped lunch today.

I open the container and stare at the well-carved fruit. My stomach rumbles again as I eye the orange strips like they're slices of prime Wagyu beef. Maybe just a bite wouldn't hurt.

I grip one piece and bring it up to my nose. I smell it, and the familiar scent floats through my sinuses. My mother used to place cantaloupe on the table every weekend morning. It was a breakfast staple. My love for the fruit is two-parts flavor and one-part memories.

I take a bite, savoring the juice before some spills from the corner of my mouth. Once I finish the strip in my hand, I notice a tang of something salty in the final bite. Something a bit... not fruity.

With a sour expression, I stare at the strips of cantaloupe and realize what a mistake I might have made. If I get sick—or worse, if I fucking die—I want proof that he was the cause.

I grab a small plastic bag from the closet and dump the container's remaining contents inside. I'll wash the Tupperware and return it at our next meeting. He doesn't have to know I didn't eat all of it. Next, I scrawl a quick note on a Post-it and attach it to the bag.

Unethical

> *If something happens to me, check this fruit. It came from Maxim Jankowski.*

Once I've placed the bag into my desk drawer, I sit back and rub my forehead. A light headache taps at my temples. This is what I get for trusting him. For being nice. Now I'll have to spend the next forty-eight hours wondering if every ache and pain is a symptom of some random poison.

Maybe Maxim has the right idea after all. Trust no one. It's safer that way.

Chapter Thirteen

Maxim

Dr. Reeves enters her house with a scowl on her beautiful face and evident frustration in every motion. I'm certain she didn't enjoy my gift at all. What a shame. I made it just for her, and it was perfect.

She carries the empty Tupperware beneath her arm, and my cock throbs at the thought of her eating that cantaloupe, her dainty fingers gripping the fruit and the puzzled look on her face when tasting the secret ingredient. My fantasy devours all that my mind conjured up and spilled for her.

She closes her front door, blows a chunk of hair away from her face, and heads toward the kitchen. My little doctor is frustrated. And angry. Is this because of me? Did she figure out my secret? Does she know my come filled her mouth?

Maybe the answer to each question is yes, and maybe she's upset with herself because she liked it. This is what I choose to believe. That she liked it and wants more, and she hates herself for it.

I wish I could go inside and take advantage of that hatred. I could fuck that hate right out of her.

But what I choose to believe isn't the same as what is real. In reality, she's probably frustrated with her fucking job, not me. She probably isn't thinking about me at all. I've guaranteed I'll creep into her brain, though. She'll try to fight it, but I'll flitter across her mind for a moment when she sets down that Tupperware container, and that's what I have to focus on. I can still infiltrate her thoughts.

That won't be enough forever, unfortunately. I'll eventually need to infiltrate *her*.

The lights flick on in a luminous trail as she travels through her house. First her kitchen light, then her dining room, and last, her living room. The nearly wall-to-wall and floor-to-ceiling windows in the living room give me a perfect view. I hurry to the back of the house and sink behind the bushes in front of my favorite oak tree so that I can continue watching her.

She slips off her coat and sits down on the couch, breaking her normal routine. She usually heads upstairs for a shower as soon as she's finished her lighting ritual. I've never seen my beautiful creature of habit relax after work.

She grabs the remote from the coffee table, flicks on the TV, and sinks into the plush couch. A contented sigh escapes her, lifting and lowering her chest as she kicks up her feet. Seeing her so relaxed feels weirder than watching her strip for a shower. Somehow, this is much more intimate. Her sudden show of normalcy intrigues me.

In our most vulnerable moments, thoughts of being watched often filter through our minds. It's human nature. Natural instinct. But when we let our guard down, when

Unethical

we're just doing normal things, we don't stop to consider who might be lurking just outside our windows.

This also means the doctor isn't thinking of me right now, and that's a problem. Am I so easily forgotten because she didn't have a full hour of me in her office? Is that why she didn't shower after work? Is she more relaxed without me?

Fuck that. She'd better learn how to relax around me. If she can't, I know how to *make* her relax.

I remain in the bushes until I realize she's nodded off. Her head slumps to the side, and the remote barely dangles from her loosened grip. Her chest moves up and down in a slow, steady rhythm. As much as I'd love to remain here and watch her sleep, I have a more exciting idea.

Through the lengthening shadows, I creep to the back of her house. The back door opens when I tug the handle, and I quietly slip inside. I could take this moment to go into the living room and take what I've always wanted, but I don't want it like that, even though I think about it almost nonstop. Instead, I climb the steps on silent feet and stand in the doorway of her bathroom.

I inhale the scent that fills my head every time I watch her shower. I step into the room and walk beside the granite countertop, trailing my fingertips over the cold surface. My hands graze all that makes her who she is.

Her brush.

Hair clips.

The hair tie she wears on her wrist.

Her fucking toothbrush. Oh god, it's perfect.

Before I even realize what I'm doing, I grab the toothbrush and whip out my cock. My hand drives my strokes as I lean over the white bristles and pleasure myself to the thought of what I'd do to her if I unleashed the monster that lurks inside me. A detailed fantasy plays in my head like a movie, and she's the unwilling star.

I spread her pretty little thighs and fuck her until she begs me to stop. I can almost taste the salt of the tears dripping from her eyes. Each imagined scream of protest sends an ache into my balls.

I stroke harder and faster as I pull the toothbrush closer and press it against the head of my cock. I spill my load on the bristles with a groan I'm forced to stifle, but some of it drips onto my hand.

That won't do.

Instead of allowing a drop to go to waste, I look for somewhere else to leave it. I glance in her shower and see a purple pouf dangling from a clear hook. The same purple pouf I've watched her rub across her naked body as she showers. I grip it and wrap my come-soaked hand around it, swiping and wiping until the last of my pleasure mixes with the mesh. I can't wait for my doctor to brush her teeth and wash her perfect body with my come.

"Enjoy having me all over your body, doc," I whisper.

As I leave the house, a sinking feeling comes over me. These little acts are losing their rush. The dopamine hit has shrunk to a negligible level, and I know it's only a matter of time before I'll need something more. Something bigger. Bolder.

Something like what I imagined in her bathroom.

While I don't want what happens between us to be entirely one-sided, while I want her to want it as much as I do, she may not give me any choice. Whether the dish is warmed up or frigid, a hungry man still needs to eat.

Chapter Fourteen

Sarah

My day starts with a sour taste in my mouth. I forgot to brush my teeth last night when I collapsed in bed. I'd been too exhausted to even turn off the bathroom light. The taste was clearly some psychosomatic flashback to the fruit, because I end up tasting it again as I brush my teeth. I toss my toothbrush in the tiny bin beneath the sink and gargle with mouthwash to get rid of that weird flavor that seems to linger.

With minty-clean breath, I force myself to go for a run. It's been months since I took the winding ATV paths behind my house and got in a good workout. I've gained ten pounds, and I feel shittier overall.

It doesn't help that I'm so miserable at my job. Maybe I wouldn't feel so bad if I actually got out of the house more often and allowed the dopamine to flow through my brain.

I close the door behind me and loop around my house toward the trees. It's nice out today, and much cooler than it has been. As I stop beside the tree line, I dust off my fitness watch and wrap it around my wrist. My pulse appears on the screen, flashing a perma-stressed ninety beats per minute.

Once I've checked that my shoes are tied tight, I head through the archway of leaves and surround myself with towering trees. I start with a slow jog. My body hardly seems to remember that I used to do two miles a day before I started my own practice.

The trees blur as I pick up speed. Shades of green meld together until they look like they belong to one gigantic plant. My breathing picks up as my feet slam into the soft soil beneath my shoes. Every additional pound I've gained weighs heavily on me as I try to run, and I'm finally forced to stop.

I place my hands on my knees and bend at the waist, blowing everything from my lungs to stop the painful stitch running up my side. As I try to catch my breath and slow my racing heart, the hair on the back of my neck prickles. I assume it's from the sweat, so I reach toward my neck to wipe it away, but the prickling sensation only spreads down my arms.

Now I'm suspicious. I feel watched.

I stop and turn on my heels, looking at the woods behind me, but aside from the trees, I see only a rogue chipmunk bouncing across the path.

Calm down.

I'm in the middle of the woods. The biggest threat to me is some rabid rabbit or something. I chuckle to myself at the thought of punting some crazed, fang-bearing bunny through the trees after it charges at me.

"Get a hold of yourself," I whisper before taking off at a slower jog.

It doesn't work.

Unethical

When I'm running, I usually obsess over every footfall and each burning sensation in my thighs, but right now I can't stop thinking about feeling watched by someone. I slow to a stop and turn around again. There's nothing. In fact, there's absolutely less than nothing. Not even a chipmunk scurries across the path.

When I turn back around, a hand clamps over my mouth. I try to scream, but my assailant's palm swallows the sound. A rubbery texture slides against my cheek as the man leans forward. The strong scent of latex wafts from his mask. It's a full skull mask, covering everything to keep me from seeing his eyes, his hair color—anything that could identify him.

Oh god, this is how I die.

That's what I get for going on a fucking run. Has binge watching *Law and Order* taught me nothing?

I shift my weight and send my sneaker into his kneecap. His leg buckles, and he releases me for a microsecond, but it's not enough time to escape. It's enough time to scream, though, and I suck in a breath and shout for help the moment his hand leaves my mouth.

He grips my arm and yanks me backward.

"What do you want from me?" I ask, fighting to pull each word from my panicked, breathless body.

A muffled voice comes from behind the mask. "Every-fucking-thing. I want everything from you."

"Please don't," I beg as the tips of his fingers dig into my skin.

He pushes me toward a tree, and my back slams against it. The fear chokes me. My fitness watch blares with a constant barrage of beeps as my pulse peaks at terrifying levels when his hand goes over my mouth again.

With his other hand, he grabs my wrist and twists. "I

love that I can see just how your body reacts to fear. You're so scared, aren't you? Afraid of what I'll do to you. Your mind is racing, too. Are you wondering if I'll fuck you?"

How do I even answer that? Of course I'm afraid. I psychoanalyze men who've done these things and have these disgusting thoughts when they see a woman alone. Men who can't control their impulses.

I want to put on my therapist cap and talk to this man as if he were a patient, but I can't. My vocal cords are frozen. The words are stuck too far down, and all I can do is nod as tears stream down my face and drip onto my chest.

"Don't worry, I'm not going to fuck you," he says.

A breath of relief blows out from instinct, but then he pins my wrists above my head. The rough bark rakes the backs of my hands.

"Don't talk or make a sound. Don't scream unless it's from pleasure. If you can't follow directions, I'll slit your throat and leave you to bleed out right here." The words struggle to overpower the frantic beeps blaring from my watch.

I nod and he removes his hand from my mouth before turning his attention to my leggings. He bunches the slick material in a tight grasp before ripping the fabric down my thighs. When I consider screaming and begging him to stop, his threats silence me.

His hand lands at the juncture between my legs and before I can even react, two of his fingers plunge inside me. I gasp and release a silent cry, but his threat tightens my throat and keeps me from screaming. He pulls his fingers from me and then plunges back inside again. And again. He continues this onslaught until my eyes roll back against my will.

"Fuck, you're tight," he growls.

His words get to me. His touch gets to me. He fucks me with his fingers and then draws out to swirl my clit before pushing inside me again. A rebellious moan escapes my lips, and I can almost sense his smirk beneath that mask.

"Are you enjoying a masked stranger fucking your sweet, innocent cunt? You're a bad girl." His muffled words are like delicate strings, and they pull tight until my pelvis curls and pushes my heat against his palm. He grinds the meat of his hand against me as he moves his fingers inside me.

Guilt swarms me like bees. Each stinging thought stabs into me with a jolt.

This feels so good.

This is so wrong.

I'm going to come.

I'm going to come to a psychopath's touch.

In the back of my mind, I know something more will follow this. Masked rapists don't just make their victims come before running off into the woods.

Just enjoy this moment, I tell myself. *When was the last time someone touched you? Wanted you? When was the last time you didn't feel so alone?*

I buck my hips against him, gyrating my pelvis to chase the sort of orgasm I haven't experienced in a long time. I snatch hold of that pleasure and selfishly ride it until my muscles contract at a dizzying pace and a wave of warmth rushes my brain. As his erection presses against the inside of my thigh, I spasm around his hand and scream out.

"You're coming for me? Dirty fucking girl," he says, his low, gravelly voice hidden behind the rubber.

As the orgasm wanes, I suck in air and lean against the tree. He pulls his hand from me and lifts his mask enough to slip his fingers beneath. Then he does something that sends another jolt of heat through my core.

He licks and sucks me off his fingers.

A low groan mixes with the wet sounds of his mouth as he tastes me. Then, without saying another word, he struts away from me with the confidence of someone deranged.

Once he's out of sight, my legs find the strength to run again. I mentally note every feature I can think of in case I call the police, but what would I even say to them? A mentally ill man in a mask just cornered me in the woods and fingered me until I came?

Jesus Christ, I wouldn't believe me, so how could I expect anyone else to?

I race into my house, lock the door behind me and, with an uncomfortable wetness between my legs, continue thinking about that man's fingers inside me.

I've been assaulted.

I was attacked.

But why was the attack so one-sided?

And will it happen again?

Chapter Fifteen

Maxim

My knee fucking hurts. She got me good. I'll admit that. But I couldn't let her go once I had her in my grasp and could smell the scent of her desperation or hear the sound of her fear.

Beep, beep, beep.

I force myself to walk normally as I step into her office. The pain grinds my kneecap, and I try to pretend it doesn't as I force the joint to work as it should. I release a breath as I sit down on the couch without drawing her gaze, but I'm not sure she'd have noticed me if I had limped in. She's staring off into space.

Did I do that to her?

I clear my throat, and she finally looks at me. "Maxim," she whispers, reaching back to grab her notepad and pen. She sets them on her lap and stares at the blank pages without looking up at me.

Yeah, I did this.

Selfishly.

Unapologetically.

She's lost in a tortured mind, and maybe it's poetic justice. Maybe she's getting a taste of what it's like. Instead of analyzing the damaged goods, she's received a little damage herself. Trauma has been forced upon her, and she just has to endure it and somehow function normally in life.

"What do you want to talk about?" I ask.

She doesn't respond.

I smirk and lower my voice. "I killed them all."

She still doesn't react to my confession.

"I pushed my brother into the well."

Nothing. She's absolutely lost in her head.

Against the pain, I get up and move toward her. She jumps when I tower over her.

"What's the matter, doc? You missed everything I said. I thought that's what you've always wanted from me."

"What'd you say?" she asks, swiping her sweat-damp hair from her cheek as she's thrust into the current moment. She still avoids my gaze, but at least she's listening.

"It's too late, doc. I'm not repeating myself. You missed some doozies, though."

I clear my throat, and she jolts. She's so jumpy. Scared. I did that. I fucking did it.

And I'll undo it.

The only way to fix the trauma I caused her is to show her there's nothing to fear from me. Not like that, at least. But if I admit I was the masked man who made her come, she'll run. Not only will she run, but she'll get away because of my bum fucking knee.

I'll have to tell her eventually, but it won't be today. Instead, I inhale her scent and allow the memories to flood back to me. How her pussy squeezed and spasmed around my fingers as she came. How pretty her little cunt was. Her moan and the scream that came from those plump lips as her body betrayed her.

I take a step to the side so the back of her chair can hide my erection. "Tell me what's bothering you."

"It's not appropriate to—"

"Do you think I care about what's appropriate?"

She swallows. "I was assaulted yesterday, Maxim. And I don't want you near me like this," she says, gaining her voice and raising her chest at me. I notice each subtle movement of her body.

My hand goes to her chin, and she jumps as I grip it. I move her head from one side to the other. "Where were you hurt?" I ask, though I know I didn't hurt her. I did the opposite of hurting her. I pleased her until she came around my fingers.

Her cheeks flush, and she grabs my wrist and tries to pull my hand away from her face. "Let go of me. You can't see where he hurt me."

Trying not to favor my leg, I stroll around the chair and end up in front of her. I lean down, not caring about my obvious erection now.

Her eyes focus on it. She opens her mouth to say something, but I speak first.

"You should probably go home and take care of yourself, doc. You're in no condition to psychoanalyze anyone else when you're so fucked up." I release her face and straighten my spine.

"Maxim," she says, sternness in her voice.

"Take care of yourself," I tell her again, leaving no room for her objection. "And count today as a full session."

Her lips part, but she swallows her words. She's going to be a good girl and file this as a full session. She's going to process what happened in those woods and come back braver than ever. She's going to come back ready for me. As much as I'd love to take advantage of her vulnerability, I want the doc that fights me, not the one who's breaking in front of me.

I won't tell her I'll see her next week, because I don't plan to wait for our next session to see her. Instead, I lean down and smirk at her. "See you soon."

Chapter Sixteen

Sarah

I brush my teeth before bed, feeling more myself today than I did yesterday. I forced myself to take the day off after Maxim, of all people, made me take time to myself. His erection has not been forgotten, but I've been too tired to acknowledge it further.

Besides, he seems like a guy who would get off on your anguish, and I was really struggling by then. Maybe I'll say something about it next week. What the hell would I even say, though?

Hey, Maxim. I noticed you had an erection last week.

Gag. I would rather pretend I didn't see it at all.

I turn off the light in the bathroom, climb into my welcoming bed, and sink beneath the down comforter. I've spent most of the day like this, but I think that's exactly what I needed. I sure as shit wasn't going for another run, that's for sure.

As my head hits the pillow, I can't stop thinking about that exact thing, though. That run. What it turned into. My hands begin to shake as I relive the memory, and I interlace my fingers over my belly to control the tremble. It's been on my mind a lot, playing on repeat.

The terrifying mask.

The way he touched me.

The way my body responded to him.

Jesus, that's what I keep focusing on the most. If I was so scared, if I truly didn't want it, how did I come?

You know better, I argue with myself.

If anyone should know that victims' bodies betray themselves all the time, it's me. It's a completely normal phenomenon, and I've explained that to clients more times than I can count. It's not my fault I went for a run. It's not my fault I was attacked. I keep chanting that on repeat in my mind.

I keep saying it until I fall asleep.

A SOFT WARMTH hovers between my legs. A curtain of heat drapes me, over and over. I blink awake, wrapped up in a tired haze. I can't orient myself in this darkness, and I feel like I'm stuck in a dream. I try to roll over, but I'm locked in from the waist down.

Yeah, it's gotta be some kind of dream. Half-body sleep paralysis coupled with lucid dreaming or some shit.

Instead of floating and feeling weightless, I'm weighed down and stuck to my mattress. I make a mental note to look up the meaning of this kind of dream. It probably means that my life is a fucking mess.

That warmth draws my attention again. A soft moan rises into my throat and rolls over my lips. I reach down to feel the source of the warmth my brain has conjured up in this dream, and my fingertips meet with slack plastic. The scent of latex wafts from beneath the blankets, bringing me back to the woods.

I'm not dreaming, I'm having a fucking nightmare.

"Wh-what?" I whisper, trying to sit up.

Hands hook my hips and keep me in place. "Shh, it's just a bad dream," he growls. "Now let me make it better."

That warmth is back on me, but I can't see him. I can't even see my fucking hand in front of my face. He's a demon lurking in the darkness and hanging on to me. But then I realize what's causing the warm pleasure between my legs.

It's his mouth, and he's eating me out. No . . . he's *devouring* me.

Now I know I'm not dreaming anymore. There's a real psychopath between my legs. But why is my brain telling me to just lie there and pretend there's not a criminal, *the* criminal, between my legs again? I'm a slut for the rising pleasure radiating from my crotch, driving into my spine, and twisting like a snake coiling in my gut.

"Please," I beg, my mouth wanting to scream for him to stop but my brain begging me to let him continue.

My body misses his tongue the moment it leaves me. "Please what?"

Tell him to stop.
Tell him to keep fucking going.
I'm so conflicted. So confused.

He waits for me to speak, swirling his fingers around my opening before plunging them inside me. I gasp, and it pushes away every word until I have none to say to him. He pistons inside me, harder and faster, until there's no way I can speak, even if I wanted to.

I scream out, my back leaving the mattress and curving

toward the ceiling. He smirks against my skin before he spreads his lips and tongues me again. Now his fingers are inside me as his tongue works my clit. My hands grip the sheets in trembling fists.

"Oh god," I pant.

My hips scoop forward and push my pussy against his mouth, begging for him to keep going.

If I reached over and turned on the light, I could see the half of his face his raised mask has left exposed. I could tell who this monster is. But instead of hitting that switch, I force him deeper into my pussy. I moan, throwing back my head as I've never felt something so good, so terribly wrong.

"Come for me," he whispers, his mouth moving against me.

His fingers dig into my thighs as he eats me until I teeter on the ledge of an orgasm. His words, the hunger in every flick of his tongue, shove me over the side. I come, gripping his head as I raise my chest and ride through the most intense orgasm I've ever had.

As soon as I come down, rational thinking plows back into my mind. I take my hand away and go for the light switch. Somehow, he knows my move, and he's on me before I reach it. He's between my legs now, over me, with my hands pinned above my head.

"I thought you were going to be a good girl, but then you went for the light," he hisses, and my wetness drips from his chin and onto my face. He's so close that I can smell my arousal coating his skin. But I can't see him. I can't see anything.

"I'm sorry," I whisper.

"I'm leaving in the darkness. If you touch that light switch before you hear that front door close, I'll come back

Unethical

next time you fall asleep, and I'll kill you and wear your blood instead of your come. Do you understand?"

"I understand."

And just like that, his warm body leaves and I'm alone with a cold heaviness. My bedroom door opens and closes. My front door opens and slams. When he's gone, when I'm *sure* he's gone, I turn on the bedroom light and look at the wet stain soaking the sheets. All that pleasure is from him waking me up with his tongue on me. From yet another assault that my body betrayed me over.

The encounter leaves me with two questions. Did I want to turn on the light to see a man I wanted more from? Or did I hope to find out who he was so I could call the goddamn police?

I don't have an answer.

Chapter Seventeen

Maxim

I grip the steering wheel and think about last night. It was ballsy of me to sneak into her home and take her cunt with my mouth, but I wouldn't take it back. I loved making my therapist come on my tongue. The therapist who hates everything about me and dreads each and every week she has to see me.

But she only hates me until I'm between her legs. When I'm there, she squirms for me.

My cock hardens, and I rub my hand over my jeans, pressing against my length. I can't stop thinking about those sounds she made and the way she clenched and twitched from pleasure. I want to feel that around my cock more than anything. I'm blind with that need.

I can't help but wonder what she'd have done if I unzipped my pants and offered her the dicking she needed just as badly. Would she have let me slip inside her soaked cunt? Would I have been able to fill her like I filled that fruit?

Fuck.

I can't go to my appointment with this rock-hard ache between my legs. I look around the lot and pull out my cock when I see no one around. My fingers glide up and down the sensitive skin as I relive last night.

I finger-fucked her in the woods the night before a session too. I wanted to see her agony face to face. Now, I want to see it again. The confused anguish as she thinks about me just as much as I think of her. Only, it's not me she's thinking of. It's the man in the mask. Her boogeyman.

I stroke myself as I think about her sweet moans. Her trembling thighs on the sides of my head. I imagine fucking her, tearing her open for my selfish pleasure. Ripping her apart. She dangles in front of me, and I don't know how much longer I can wait for her to give it up to me willingly. She doesn't have to, of course, but I would love to see that same torn hunger that I felt on my tongue last night.

I come with a groan, catching it in my hand, then bringing my palm to my mouth and closing my eyes as I tongue my flesh the same way I lapped at her pussy. With long, driven strokes, I clean myself off so I can go into that little office and try to talk about my past. I swallow the salty, slick come and wipe a drop from my lower lip before smirking at myself in the rearview mirror.

"Showtime, doc," I whisper, brushing my hair from my face with my clean hand.

I get out of the car and head into the office, careful not to wipe the last bit of residue off my palm. The bell above the entrance goes off as soon as I walk in, announcing to the otherwise empty office that I've arrived. I head right for the big white door at the end of the hall, the one with Dr. Sarah Reeves' placard next to it.

When I step inside, she's crying at her desk. I should

have knocked, but then I would have missed out on seeing this painful, raw emotion oozing out of her.

"Maxim, I-I'm so sorry," she stammers, wiping the tears from her face. "I can't—"

I step closer and put my hand over hers, pressing my come into her skin as I feign a human emotion that comes naturally for everyone else. It's a comforting gesture that she meets with her hand over mine.

Well, I *thought* it was comforting. She actually grips my wrist and plucks my hand off hers.

"I can't do a session today," she says.

I take a step back from her. "But what if I'm in the mood to talk, doc? What if I came in here wanting to spill all my guts for you?"

"You aren't and you didn't. We both know that." The ghosts of her tears dry on her face. I've distracted her from whatever has her so upset, at least.

Believe it or not, I don't love seeing her cry, even if I like being the reason she's crying. I like that she's distraught because she doesn't know what to do with her feelings about the masked man pleasing her—*me* pleasing her.

I stride toward the couch and plop down, dropping my hands to my knees before my fingers intertwine on my lap. "What do you want to know about me?"

Sarah stands and walks to the chair right across from me. She sits down. Her chin rises. I can hardly tell she was crying any longer. "I don't think you'll tell me anything that isn't a lie."

"I'll tell you a truth if you tell me why you were crying."

She scoffs but leans back in the chair. Her eyes dance around as she stares at me, as if she's trying to figure out if it's worth spilling her secret to get out one of mine. It's the only chance she has of getting that out of me, so she should take this opportunity.

"Fine," she says. "But you have to talk first."

"What do you want to know, doc?"

She circles her chin with her fingers. "Did you kill your foster parents?"

"Bold question." I lean back, my shirt riding up as I put my hands behind my head. "But yes, I did."

She blinks at me with much less of a reaction than I expected. It's because she knew that answer already. She knew all along.

"Why?" she asks.

"Ah, one question at a time. My turn. Why were you crying?"

She shakes her head. "I'm not comfortable talking about this with you."

"I'm not comfortable talking about my dead fucking foster parents with you either, but here I am. Spill."

She rolls her eyes, but they land on me again before sinking to the floor. "I think I have a stalker. And he broke into my house last night . . ." She exhales.

"What'd he do to you?" I ask, leaning forward and putting my forearms on my lap. A spark of jealousy ignites in my gut. Why the fuck am I getting jealous of myself? It was my mouth on her. My tongue that made her come. "What'd he fucking do to you?"

Her cheeks flame red at the protective bite to my tone that's even surprising to me. "Nothing," she whispers, refusing to look at me.

"Tell me, doc. What did that man do to you?"

She sighs. "He used his mouth on me."

A twisted flare of arousal eats away at that jealousy and possessiveness as she tells me what I did to her.

"So you're telling me someone came into your room and put his mouth on you? That's not a stalker, baby, that's a boyfriend."

"There's this thing called consent, Maxim."

"Did you tell him you didn't want it? Better yet, *did* you want it?"

Her lips tighten. "God, why would I expect you to understand why I'm upset? I was crying because I'm frustrated. Because I know no one will believe me! Not even a criminal like you believes me."

Ouch, doc. "No, I believe you. I just think you're being a little overdramatic about it."

"This man put his fingers inside me. He put his mouth on me! It's assault!"

I love hearing that my fingers were the reason she was upset the first time. I can't help but wonder how much more upset she'd be if her masked stalker took her sweet little needy cunt next.

"You're right, doc." I stand up and step toward her. Placing my hands on the arms of the chair, I lean closer. "I'm sorry."

She looks up into my face, and for the first time, I don't see fear. I see defeat. So why don't I feel good about it?

"It's fine. I don't expect you to give a shit about anyone else. But I've answered the question, so now it's your turn. Why did you kill your foster parents?"

Sarah is wrong. I do care about her. I'm obsessed with her. I know what I do to her is wrong, but it's the only thing right for me now. I *need* to touch her. *Need* to please her. I care about what's happening to her, but I can't stop. My selfish desires override my emotions, and I intend on taking it to the point of no return. And then I'll have to disappear, because she can't find out it was me.

"Well?" she asks, pushing the question.

"I killed my foster parents because they were abusive pricks who didn't deserve to draw air."

"In what ways were they abusive?"

I shake my head. "Back and forth, remember? Answer my earlier question. When that man put his mouth on you, did you want it? Did you come on his tongue?"

Anger simmers through her veins, making her cheeks flush. I'm so close that I can feel the heat rising from her skin. "Get the fuck out of my office, you sadistic asshole! You like getting a rise out of me, don't you? You—"

Her fire-soaked lips are so close to mine, and she's throwing every heated syllable right at me. I'm tethered to those lips, and the string pulls taut. I lean into them and burn from the heat of her anger.

Her lips begin to move, but then she stops and pulls her head away. "Maxim, no," she says, the sternness filling the space between those two words.

I don't want her to realize that the man she's crying over and the man attached to her face are the same, so I pull away.

"Sorry," I say. "I read the room wrong."

"What about any of this said to kiss me?" she snaps, wiping me off her lips as if I'm dirty. "Don't ever do that again."

Then she gazes up at me and something very unexpected happens. She leans forward and kisses me back.

Chapter Eighteen

Sarah

I stand in my kitchen and absently stir noodles as my tormented mind circles, dissects, and lays bare the most insane thing I've ever done in my entire life.

I. Fucking. Kissed. Maxim.

I leaned in and pressed my lips to the mouth of an absolute sociopath. My client. And this was *after* he came clean about committing murder. Why did I do that?

I have no idea, and I can't begin to psychoanalyze myself right now. We had a moment. A singular moment where I forgot who he was and who he was to me. I'm his fucking *therapist*.

But when he was standing there, his eyes boring into my soul and his warm lips still a recent memory of mine, I could only think of how he looked in front of me. How he stole a kiss from me first. I *liked* feeling wanted, just like I did on the trail behind my house. And in my bed. Maxim was present in a weak moment, that's all. That's it.

Right?

A tendril of steam whips across my skin, and I rip my hand away from the pan. This has to stop. These people are infiltrating my mind and infecting me with their psychosis, and if I'm not more careful, I'll succumb to my own version of mental illness. Maybe I already have. Hell, I was wanton enough to come on my stalker's face and kiss a known felon in my place of employment.

I sigh and drop my head to my hands. My place of employment. My livelihood! I risked it all because Maxim was riding on the coattails of a deranged madman who is hellbent on making me come. I kissed a client, all while knowing he could file a complaint about me or get my license revoked or, at the very least, have me suspended from practice. Fuck, this is all I need to add to my plate full of shit sandwiches.

I know damn well Maxim will use that kiss against me. It doesn't matter that I pulled away the moment our tongues touched, then told him this could never happen again. That sinful smirk on his face told me everything I needed to know. He won't chalk it up to a little lapse in judgment. He won't be a nice fucking person about it and understand that I was weak and hurting. He'll take the weapon I handed him and use it against me the first chance he gets.

Turn him in first, my intrusive thoughts whisper. *No one will believe him from prison.*

But that's more unethical than initiating intimate contact with a client. It's my fault I kissed him, and I can't turn him in because of my piss-poor judgment call. He might have kissed me first, but I'm a professional. I'm the responsible one.

I grip the wooden spoon and stir my dinner again.

You liked it, the intrusive thoughts say, loud and clear.

That nagging voice filters through my consciousness and forces me to confront my actions head on.

Yes. I liked kissing him. I wanted to keep going. I wanted to take it further. But I couldn't. We can't. If I had met Maxim outside of work, this wouldn't be a problem, but our situation is what it is and it can't be changed. His deranged ass walked into my office and took a fucking seat.

I lower the spoon again and put my back against the edge of the counter. The warmth from the stove radiates toward my left side, but a different heat radiates from somewhere else.

My hand eases toward my pencil skirt and slips beneath the waistband, finding the wetness that gathered within the warmth. Thinking about Maxim isn't helping me stay ethical. I trespass back into another forbidden landscape as I rub my fingers between my slit to thoughts of him. I lean back and stroke tightening circles over my sensitive clit to what never happened in the office.

What if he hadn't listened to my "no"? What if his hand went to my throat and he pushed me back against the wall? What if he kept kissing me? What if his mouth went lower? His hands? What if they drove up my skirt and he fucked me right there in my office?

Moans softly pour from my lips. I don't stop these thoughts. I let them run rampant. I let them ravage me until my heart thumps against my chest and my breathing grows ragged. My muscles tighten and tense.

My dinner is burning on the stove, but I don't care. As the smoke alarm blares, I spread my thighs a bit, drop the back of my head against the cabinet, and let myself come to the thoughts of Maxim railing me. Demolishing me. Making me his.

As soon as I come, as soon as the brilliant high wears off,

I turn off the stove and run to the bathroom. I vomit up bile and my ethics as I stare at my come-coated fingers wrapped around the rim of the toilet. I'm absolutely horrified and disgusted by my thoughts and the fact that I'm going to places I would never have dared dream of before Maxim. Places where my core values are burned in a pit carved by my sinful desires.

"Oh fuck," I whisper.

The smoke alarm continues screaming, almost an omen of what's going on in my head. Alarms mean you need to run, to get out, and that's what I should be doing. But here I am, coming in the flames instead.

Chapter Nineteen

Maxim

It's the day before our session, which means . . . Well, it means I'm spoiling myself with another date Sarah doesn't know she's having. Has she begun to expect me by now? I saw her rubbing herself in the kitchen when I was watching through the window, and I can't help but wonder if she was thinking about me.

Someone certainly filled her thoughts and distracted her from her meal. Someone filled her with such need that she had to throw everything aside to get herself off.

God, I hope it was me.

But even if it was, she'd never admit it.

I came with her that day, and I haven't stopped thinking about her since. I've been eager to get my hands on her, but I had to wait for the day before our appointment. I want to give her some time to come to terms with what happened between her and her masked stranger. Tonight, I'll make her question everything about herself.

Once nighttime comes and I'm certain she's getting

ready for bed, I sneak to her back door. That's where I want to catch her this time. The first time, I bathed in her fear as much as her pleasure. The second time, I lived in her confused surprise. This time, I want her to be awake when I show up. I can't wait for her to realize that tonight isn't just about her. I'm going to get mine as well. I'll finally feel what I've rabidly fantasized about for so long.

My hand isn't enough anymore.

The door squeals as it slides along the track, and then my boots hit the mat covering the tile dining room floor. After I woke her up with my tongue, you'd think she'd have locked up or gotten cameras, but she hasn't. Or none that I can see, at least. Maybe it's because she subconsciously wants me to return.

I drop my mask in place and head for the stairs. I cushion every step as I try to keep the risers from squeaking beneath my weight. When I get to her room at the end of the hall, I wait outside, trying to steady my breathing. No isn't an answer tonight. My cock aches for the one thing I can't have.

Her.

I open the door, and she's sitting up in bed. Her eyes rise to mine without the fear and shock I hope for. She was expecting me. She won't admit it, but she was waiting for me.

Unfortunately for me, her phone sits in her outstretched hand. She's pressed the numbers to call 9-1-1, and the phone is simply waiting for her to press the call button.

"Are you going to call them?" I ask.

Her finger hovers over the green button on the screen. "Depends."

"On what?"

"What you plan on doing to me."

Unethical

I lean against the doorway and cross my legs. "I want you. All of you. If you don't plan on giving it to me, go ahead and make that call."

Her thumb quivers over the button before her shoulders drop. I kick off the wall and cross the room until I'm right in front of her. I put a hand around her throat, lift her, and push her against the wall. Her breath hitches, but she keeps a firm grip on the phone.

I expect her to hit the call button, but instead, her grip loosens and she lets the phone fall to the floor. Without exchanging words, I put my hand down her black shorts. She's soaked. How long has she been waiting for me? Hoping for me to show up?

I rip down the fabric and let it fall, like her abandoned phone. Her cheeks flush as I strip her down to nothing but the cami she intended to sleep in. I unbutton and unzip my jeans, pulling my cock through the splayed fabric, then lift her leg as I push my body into her. My fingertips sear the backs of her thighs as I hold my cock against the pussy I pretty much dreamed of for the last month.

"Tell me to fuck you," I growl. "Tell me you want the monster who breaks into your home and violates you to rip open your tight little pussy."

"I won't tell you that," she whispers.

"You can't tell me. Because if you come on my dick, that's the ultimate sin, isn't it?"

She nods, tears welling in the corners of her eyes. She's going to hate herself afterward. I know that. But I know damn well she's going to love it while I'm inside her. She can't let herself want me. Not the masked version of me or the real one.

I draw back my hips, letting my cock slip down to her entrance. I thrust forward, pushing inside her. She screams as I selfishly bury myself to the hilt inside her. Her warm wetness tightens around me. Almost too tight. I can't control the groan that rushes from my lips as she envelops all of me.

She's so much better than my hand. Or the fruit. She's better than anything I could ever imagine.

I put my hand on the wall beside her head and thrust harder and faster, slamming her against the wall behind her. She screams out, and it's not from pleasure at first, but those sounds change as I grind my hips against her between every thrust.

"Be a good girl and rub yourself," I growl against her ear. "Make yourself come for me."

I'd rub her myself, but I need my hand to keep her open for me. My fingertips dig into the back of her thigh from the pleasure she's strangling out of me. And besides, I want her to drag that pleasure out of herself. For me. I want her to say *fuck you* to her morals as she rubs that pretty cunt. I want her to play with herself like she did in the kitchen.

I want to know what it feels like to be inside her when she comes.

She reaches between us, and her hand rocks as she rubs herself. Her head drops back as the pleasure builds and burns inside her. She looks so pretty as she lets down her walls and allows herself to feel good. Her teeth bite into her lower lip as she tries to keep the sounds at bay, but I want to hear them.

"Scream all you want," I say.

Her muffled whimpers turn to screams as she bears down on me. I can feel how close she is, like Morse fucking code.

"That's it, come for me."

Her body twitches and jerks as she loses her balance from the pleasure. I take my hand from the wall and lift her

Unethical

instead, wrapping both of her legs around my waist. Her thighs tremble against me as she brings herself to the edge and I fuck her over it.

She comes, her head thrown back in unstifled pleasure. It's fucking beautiful. She spasms around me, trying to pull an orgasm from me too.

"Don't come inside me," she pants.

I have no choice but to listen to her. This time, at least. As this masked man, I ride a delicate line between pleasing her and being her villain. But I will fill her. Maybe not tonight. But soon. I need to claim her. To make her mine.

For now, I drop her to her feet and push her to her knees. She looks up at me as I stuff my cock into her mouth. I fuck her face until the urge to come crawls toward my head. I pull out of her mouth and spill my load on her face, spreading the white cream across her lips and cheeks. The guilt and regret wash over her features as soon as I cover her with everything her sexy little cunt drew from me.

I slap her cheek, smearing my come into her skin, and then I turn to leave.

She wipes her face with a heavy hand. "Please don't come back," she snips, the weight of what happened weighing heavily on her now. "You got what you wanted."

I shake my head and grip the doorknob. I may have gotten what I wanted this time, but she keeps making me want more. Stopping now isn't an option.

Chapter Twenty

Sarah

I sit on my bed and try to process what just happened. I ache between my legs from yet another assault. No, I'm not allowed to call it that. I let him fuck me, and now I have to deal with the emotional aftermath.

The encounter weighs heavily on me now, grinding me into dust from the pressure. A cyclone of emotions twists inside me. My love and hate hold my hands and spin with me in this confusing storm. I enjoyed the pleasure and desire, but I hate him for what he did to me before. In the woods.

The fear isn't a distant memory. It's still so fresh in my mind. Even though he makes me come, he's not a good person. Good people don't break into homes, no matter if their intent is to give pleasure or hurt someone. He's a terrible, dangerous man.

And I let him inside me.

Oh god, what did I do? What did I allow to happen? I knew he was coming tonight, or maybe it was just wishful thinking, but some nervous, excited feeling coursed through me as each minute ticked by and he hadn't broken into my house again to please me.

It's been so long since I've been intimate with anyone that it made me deranged, I guess. He's made me crave a man who can't even show his face to me. A man who left as soon as he was done using me, not once, but three times now.

What am I doing?

And why would I do it again?

Desperation is a horny bitch, it seems.

I cleaned off my face, but his orgasm lingers on my skin long after he finished spilling it on my cheeks. It burns me like a brand, as does the phantom touches where he grazed my stomach, my thighs. The places he touched feel like they don't belong to me anymore. I'm no longer my own person. He snatches parts of me with each encounter, claiming them as his. If this keeps happening, I'll lose myself completely.

I throw my face into the pillow and scream. I'm so mad at myself for reveling in the touch of a psychopath. I'm also angry with myself for being so stupid because a man with a big dick decided to stalk and harass me. This is so unlike me. Before Maxim, I never would have—

Maxim.

What if it's him? What if he's the masked man who stalks and assaults me?

I shake my head. I would know if he'd been the man making me come. He'd probably call me doc if it were him.

Even though he isn't the masked stranger, he's still a problem. He planted a seed of darkness in my brain, and now it's tainting my morality while I let the masked man take advantage of me. That psycho reaps the benefits of the darkness sown by Maxim.

Is this who I've become? Or is this who I've always been but fought so hard to not become? Have I helped so many unhinged people because I'm actually pretty unhinged myself?

They say it takes one to know one. Maybe I'm not the pure soul I try so hard to portray myself as. A morally righteous person wouldn't fuck a masked stranger like I have, though. They definitely wouldn't have come from it.

And there's no fucking way they'd hope for more.

The desire to feel wanted and needed is both intoxicating and dangerous. I'm playing jump rope with a saw blade at this point. The adrenaline sends me on a high with each pass of the whirring circle of sharp teeth, but it will eventually chop me off at the knees.

I walk to the living room and flop onto the couch. My eyes close, and I begin to analyze myself. This need to feel desired springs from somewhere. I search through my childhood for some repressed memory, but I find nothing. My mind wanders through my dating history, but nothing jumps out at me.

I can only come up with one plausible answer. I chose this line of work not because I have a desire to fix my clients' messed up heads but because maybe, just maybe, they can fix mine.

Chapter Twenty-One

Maxim

How the hell am I supposed to sit here in front of her without replaying last night in my mind? How can I think of anything aside from how she sounded as she came or how she looked when my come landed on her skin?

"Hello? Maxim, are you even listening to me?" she asks, raising her voice.

"I'm going to be honest with you, doc. I'm not," I say, and her jaw drops at my bluntness.

I stand, and she notices my hard cock. I don't hide it from her, which is probably a mistake because she instinctively stands and begins inching toward her purse, which hangs from a hook on the wall.

I block her with my arm as I step into her. "I haven't listened to a word you've said because my mind is on something much more interesting."

"And what's that?" she asks.

I lean closer, and she flinches. "Do you really want to know the answer to that?"

"Maxim, think about what you're doing," she scolds, but it only turns me on even more.

"I've thought about it plenty. Mainly while I stood outside of your house."

She shakes her head. "Stop lying to me. You're just trying to get a rise out of me."

I smirk at her. "The tan Cape Cod at the very end of Maple Hill Place, right?"

She gasps, but I can't help but wonder if she's known all along that I've been following her. Doing more to her.

"That is extremely . . . inappropriate . . ." She struggles to speak, losing her intelligence in front of my eyes. In fact, she's losing her most basic instincts, and each word she speaks is as broken as I am. She could call for help. She moved up the time of our visits, and there's someone just outside that door. But she doesn't.

"Yeah, it is, but do you know what's more inappropriate? I've come so many times to you as you strip and shower." I reach out and stroke her face, and she rips away from my touch.

Her cheeks flush. "Maxim," she whispers, "I'm calling the police."

I take a step back from her. "Go on, call them."

She looks at her cellphone on the desk, then back at me, but she doesn't make a move.

"I'm giving you one chance to make the call before I make my thoughts a reality." When she remains planted where she stands, I raise an eyebrow.

"I don't think you're stupid enough to do something that will land you back in prison," she says, puffing her chest.

"You don't know me, doc. I *will* risk prison if it means I

get to be inside you." *Again*, I want to say, but I bite my tongue. I fist her hair, and she whimpers. "If you decide to call the police after I take your cunt, I'll sit in my fucking prison cell and remember how you felt when I made you come in your little office."

She blinks at me. A battle rages inside her, I'm sure. Does she let such a vile person take her, or does she use those beautiful lips to call for help?

"Only if you answer a question for me," she says, still trying to keep the upper hand.

I cock my head at her. "What question has nagged you hard enough that you'd fuck me for the answer? Do you want in my head that bad?"

She swallows. "Did you kill your brother?"

A laugh rumbles up from deep in my gut. "What a question."

My hand rides up her skirt, and her body tenses. She didn't act like this when I was in her house. When the masked stranger touched her, she practically melted. Am I that much worse than him?

When I push her panties aside, I run two fingers along her slit before pushing them inside her. Once I'm deep enough to feel her clit against my palm, I answer her.

"Yes, I pushed my brother into the well." The moment the words exit my mouth, her hand rushes to my wrist to stop me. "Ah-ah, doc. My answer for your cunt, even if it's not what you wanted to hear."

I fuck her with my fingers until her hand releases from my wrist and grips her skirt. A soft moan leaves her lips and goes right to my dick.

"There you go," I whisper as I lean my weight into her and finger her harder. "Let me make you feel good."

"Maxim," she whispers, and there's apprehension in the

word. She should be apprehensive. I'm what her textbooks warned her about in school.

With my hand still wrapped in her hair, I drag her to the place I've imagined bending her over most often: the desk. I push her chest down and keep my hand buried in her cunt.

"I feel you tightening," I growl. "Don't come yet, not until my cock is inside you." I lean my weight into her, pushing her pelvis against the wooden desk. I pull my hand from her and bring my fingers to my mouth. I taste her, and it's better than ever. The fear makes her even more delicious. She's sweet and forbidden.

I unbutton and unzip my jeans, pulling my cock from the splayed fabric. I push my cock inside her because I can't wait a second longer to feel her at this angle. She moans as I push to the depths of her. She's so goddamn tight, even more so with her legs clenched together.

I wrap an arm around her and pull her against my pelvis. Sinking into something I've wanted this fucking bad as myself, as Maxim, is indescribable. It's a similar feeling to the day I found out I was getting out of prison, but even better. I imagine it's like a pardon when you're strapped to the execution table, which is where I belong.

The strength of my thrusts knocks her against the desk, rattling everything on top of it. She moans, and I throw a hand over her mouth, drawing her up to me.

"Shh, doc," I breathe against her ear.

She throbs around me, a tightening I feel along the entire length of my dick.

"Have you ever fucked a client before me?" I ask.

She shakes her head, moving my hand with the motion.

"You could lose your license for this, huh?"

Her nod is slow and apprehensive.

"Bad, bad doc," I growl. I drop my hand from her mouth and lean over her, hitting the speakerphone button of her desk phone. The dial tone sounds beside us.

"What are you doing?" she asks, panting.

"Giving you the chance to turn me in," I say. I mark every press of the buttons with a hard thrust. The phone rings. I drop my hand between her legs and stroke her clit, and her pelvis scoops as I rub her.

"9-1-1, what's your emergency?" says a muffled voice from the speaker.

I wait for Sarah to speak. Maybe she'll remain quiet and force them to come to us. I thrust faster, grinding my pelvis against her ass as I brush her clit with the pads of my fingers. Her body trembles and tenses.

"Hello?" the speaker blares. "Do you need help?"

Sarah leans over, trying to control her breathing. "Hello, I'm Doctor Sarah Reeves. We have to dial nine and one to make calls out from my office. I must have called by mistake. I apologize for wasting your time," she says, as calmly as she can. Her professional tone excites me.

"Alright, ma'am. Are you sure you don't need emergency services?"

I fuck her through her answer.

"Very sure, have a good day," she says, wiping sweat from her forehead. The line goes dead, and the light for the speakerphone flashes off.

Good girl.

"That's so stupid," she hisses. "They still might come."

"Then I'd better hurry," I growl. "I know you want to come. So come."

She shakes her head but drops her forehead to her desk, stemming her moans with the back of her arm.

I stroke her clit until she's clenching my dick. Her

spasms squeeze me, riding up my length in waves until I get close. She comes around me, backing up, taking me deeper inside her.

"I'm going to fill your cunt, doc."

"Don't come inside me," she says as she reaches back and pushes a hand against my thigh. That masked stranger listened to her last night, but this reckless felon isn't so careful or cautious. There's no way I won't fill her this time.

I give her a final hard thrust, grinding my hips against her ass as I pour all of my evil inside the one who's tasked with fighting it. I pull out and stare as her skirt slips down her full ass. She's fucking perfect.

When she stands up and turns around, she looks at my come-coated dick, and her lips draw into a frown. "I told you not to come inside me," she snaps, but an ebb of panic infiltrates the last of her words. "And, oh god."

The gravity of what she's done and who she's fucked weighs her down. Much more than when she let herself be taken by a masked stranger.

I step into her and kick her legs apart. I catch what's dripped from her and push it back inside her with two of my fingers. Her cheeks flame red.

"You're mine, doc. Your cunt is branded with my come. If you want more of what's in my head, give me more of you." I zip up my jeans and reach for the door. "See you tonight."

Chapter Twenty-Two

Sarah

I try to cover my bathroom window with a towel, but I can't find something to hook it to. I blow out a frustrated breath and let the blood-red towel fall to the base of the windowsill. When my eyes scan the dark backyard, I don't see anything, but I get the eerie feeling he's watching me. He fucking knew where I lived, and he said he would come back for me tonight.

I made a mistake. A stupid and unethical mistake that can ruin everything I've ever worked for. As fucked up as Maxim is, something about him heats my blood. Something that makes me curious to know more. I learned too much about him, though, like how his cock feels.

But that's not the only problem. I also have this situation with the masked man who always shows up the same day. I've had such a dry spell, and now I've somehow attracted two psychopaths. What's wrong with me? Do I have *vulnerable* written across my fucking forehead or something?

I scan the ground, trying to see him hiding somewhere in the shadows, but the only movement is the wind through the trees. I can't decide if it's worse to see him out there or to know that he might be.

As a shiver rushes through me, I again try to finagle some way to block off his ability to see me. I never got curtains for this window because it faces the woods. Gripping the thick fabric, I raise it above my head and try to cram the corners into the sill, but the weight just brings it down again. This is pointless. Maybe I can cut holes into the corners and hook them over the corners of the frame.

As I grasp the towel again, the doorbell cries with a cheery tone that freezes me in my tracks, and the towel falls from my grasp once more. I walk down the stairs, heading toward the front door, and I know who waits outside.

Call the police, I tell myself. But instead of listening, I grip the doorknob and ease it open.

"Are you trying to fuck with my nightly show, doc?" Maxim says as he stands on my doorstep. "Don't be selfish."

His words infuriate me. He has some nerve. *My* privacy is not selfish. He's the selfish one. No, that word doesn't describe him well enough. He's *evil*.

"I'm calling the cops, Maxim," I say.

"Go ahead. I'll wait," he goads, crossing his arms over his chest.

I will. I'll fucking call them.

My hands refuse my demands to grab the phone, and my feet refuse to listen when I beg them to step away so we can slam the door in his face. He's so frustrating. But something in my body wants more, even when my mind doesn't.

"Didn't think so. May I come in?" He pushes past me before I can answer, then grabs my arm and tugs me toward the stairs.

I dig my heels in. "Where are you taking me?"

"You're going to shower, and I'm getting a front-row seat this time."

His strong grip is too powerful to fight. He just drags me, no matter what I grip and grab on the way up the stairs. Maxim walks me into the bathroom and locks the door before standing in front of it.

"Let me go," I say.

"I'm not doing anything to you. Just do what you usually do. Pretend I'm not even here," he says, leaning back against the door.

He's insane. Clinical. I'm not getting undressed in front of him, even if I already have and didn't know about it. Even if he's gotten a piece of my body in my office. This is different. A shower is my private time. It's my personal space.

He motions for me to go on. Fuck him. "Do you need me to get violent with you, doc? You know I'm capable of a great deal of violence."

I blow out a defeated breath because I do know.

I reach up and unbutton my silk shirt. The fabric spreads, and his eyes force their way through me, seeing into my very soul. I let the shirt fall to the ground. When I unclip my bra and let that fall, a low growl leaves his lips. I lower my skirt, but he doesn't step toward me, even when I'm naked in front of him. With caution marking every step, I climb into my shower, close the curtain, and breathe a sigh of relief against the wall. He's not gone, but at least he can't see me behind the opaque curtain.

Until it rips across the rod and he just stands beside me, his hands wrapped around the metal, staring at me.

His eyes assault me. I've never felt so picked apart by a single glare. He fucks me with them as they glide over every inch of my body.

"You're a sexy fucking thing," he growls.

"Thanks?" I say, because what else do you say to someone who compliments you under duress?

"Goodnight. I sure will have one," he says before releasing the metal bar and ripping the curtain across.

"Maxim?" I yell.

It sounds like he left, though, so I fall back against the wall, my breath halting in my chest. I'm afraid to open the curtain again. Afraid to leave the sanctity of my shower.

I finish washing up as quickly as I can and turn off the water. I slide the curtain open and look around the empty bathroom. He's definitely gone. At least from my bathroom. My clothes are also gone, though.

Goddamn it.

I wrap the towel around me, and as I tuck it into itself, I catch a glimpse of my silk shirt in the hallway, just outside the door. I follow it, finding my bra on the steps. Like Hansel and Gretel, I follow the breadcrumbs of strewn clothing. My skirt guides me toward the front door. And wrapped around the doorknob are my black panties. I pick them off and feel warm, slick wetness on the material.

He came in my fucking underwear.

Are you kidding me? Disgusting. He's vile.

So why does his warm come on my panties make my thighs clench?

Chapter Twenty-Three

Maxim

My balls are empty, unloaded on the panties that the doc had been wearing. The best part? The dried spot I saw, which came from my come inside her earlier.

Unable to stop myself, I'd let my tongue scrape against the perfect mixture of hers and mine. I tasted all of it. And nearly busted in my pants because of it. Lucky for me, her panties made an excellent place to deposit an impromptu load.

Now I'm hunkered among clothes as I watch her through a slit in her bedroom closet. She throws her come-soaked panties into a small trash can with less of a reaction than I expected—or hoped for. Then she grabs a cami and a pair of shorts from a drawer and slips into them. With a strained sigh, she sits on the edge of the bed.

Her fists clench against her thighs, and her shoulders tense. She rolls her neck, trying to relieve the pent-up strain in her muscles. I should step out of my hiding place and massage her. She'd be scared at first, but once I start rubbing her stress away, she'll beg me to keep going. Then I'd move to her lower back. And even lower. I'd rub that sweet ass of hers before burying my face between her cheeks and eating her like she's never been eaten before.

But I don't step out of the closet. I keep still and watch her.

At first, I think she'll cry after everything I've put her through today, which is probably a fair response. I've forced her to put her dignity aside and let something undignified inside her. No tears fall, though. Her eyes drop before the lids close, and she disappears inside her mind. What she does next both surprises and confuses me.

Biting her lower lip, she dips her hand beneath her shorts. My jaw drops as she leans back on the bed, her hand moving beneath the black fabric. I can't believe what I'm witnessing. Instead of shedding moisture from her pretty eyes, she's dripping from that sweet little cunt.

"Naughty doc," I whisper.

Had I known I'd get to see her like this, I'd have waited to jerk off. I can't help but wonder if she's thinking of me. Does she like it when I make her do things she doesn't want to like? Is she imagining me instead of her fingers between her legs?

Moans leave her lips, and her back arches. "Maxim," she whispers through a groan.

She answers my question with that single word and a whole lot of moans. She is. She's fucking thinking of me, the unhinged and dangerous felon she's let inside.

My cock twitches at the sight of her. Light peeks beneath the curve of her back as she lifts into the air from the pleasure she's bringing herself. The shorts tent and move as she touches herself, and I stroke the front of my pants, my dick springing to life again.

I'm half-tempted to leap from the closet like some kind of maniac and bury my face in her cunt like an animal. I'm all of those things already, so why stay leashed and in control when she's whispering my name and calling to me as she pleasures herself?

Instead, I stay hidden because I want to mark her. I pull out my dick and slowly stroke myself. The screaming moan she releases as she comes makes my dick twitch in my hand. When she sits up, her shoulders fall forward with guilt, a heaviness from what she thought about as she came.

Before she climbs into bed, she shakes a pill from a bottle on the nightstand and swallows it with a cup of water. When she gets into bed, so tired from all that's happened to her today, she draws her blanket up to her like a shield from the outside world. A shield from everything but me.

I stay in the closet until she's snoring in a deep sleep. The door creaks as I open it, and I don't try to stop it. If she wakes up, she wakes up. I'm a shadow creeping across the floor as I walk toward her bed.

The moonlight from the window casts a pale glow over Sarah's sleeping form. I continue to stroke my dick as I peel her shield away and pull back the blanket. Her ass is full, and the cuffs peek from the fabric. Fuck, she's delicious. It takes everything in me to stop myself from pulling the shorts aside and devouring her sweet little cunt.

I roll her onto her back, and now I see her face. So relaxed and sexy when she's not looking guilty from fucking the literal devil.

I'm going to come. I'm tempted to do so on her pretty little face so she'll wake up in the morning with my mark on her lips, but I want to mark her pussy more. I reach down and move her shorts aside, running a finger through her soaked slit. She made herself so wet.

Using two fingers to spread her, I stroke my dick along her clit until I come, marking her skin just like I marked her panties. I don't even know how I've managed to come three times today. I'd come a thousand times for her, though.

"Good girl," I whisper as I put her shorts back in place and leave her asleep and covered in my come.

What an absolutely vile piece of shit I am for this. She'll wonder if I fucked her while she was asleep. She'll wonder if I used her body as selfishly as I wanted to. The question is, will she like the idea or not?

Chapter Twenty-Four

Sarah

I'm trying to avoid his eyes. I feel like I've been sucking on a cotton ball, and I keep excusing myself to drink from my water bottle. He notices every move I make. His eyes are like lasers, burning into my very core.

Contrasting feelings intermingle in my gut. One sends jolts between my legs and makes me tighten my thighs. The other sends warning bells to my mind.

I'm uncomfortable. I shouldn't want to be here with him, but worse, I can't stop the thoughts I had last night as I touched myself. I have to pull myself out of this downward spiral.

I force my focus onto my work. Even though *he* is my fucking work.

My job is to rip apart his psyche and put it back together. I'm supposed to mend him instead of fuck him in my mind. Or fuck him in real life. Jesus, what am I doing?

"T-tell me about your time in prison, Maxim. Did you struggle with it, or did you adapt well?" I ask.

My voice wavers at the start, but I fall into my routine, and the rest of the sentence glides from my mouth out of habit. I love delving into how they handled being incarcerated, and I like to spend quite a bit of time unpacking those feelings that come from being inside. I tend to find that those who adapt really well to prison often had the rockiest childhoods. There's a sort of safety and comfort in the structured routine of prison. He seems like he'd be someone who would have adapted well.

"We're still doing this, doc?" he asks.

"What? My job? Yes. I have certain requirements the court demands I fulfill regarding your treatment. Certain progress that needs to be made for them to consider it successful. This is your second-to-last session with me, and we for sure haven't made that progress."

"What do you need from me?" he asks, as if he cares to give it to me.

"I need you to open up. You need to stop being this hollow shell of a person."

The hollow shell of a man who I let have sex with me. Oh god. The heavy feeling of regret punches me in the gut.

He laughs. "You don't want me to open up. I'm a bad person. The 'hollow shell' you see walls off a psycho from the rest of the world."

My mouth opens and closes. How do I even respond to this? This man admitted to being a murderer last week, and he just admitted he's capable of doing it again. I have a moral and legal responsibility to report my findings because he's a risk to others.

And he's not just a risk to others.

He's a risk to *me*.

"Stop telling me those things, Maxim," I whisper, shaking my head as I battle with myself.

"You wanted me to be open and honest, and now you want me to stop?"

I sigh. "I have a legal responsibility to report—"

"Report indecent acts?" Maxim flashes a dark grin at me. "Like fucking your client?"

"You can't use that against me," I say, lifting my chest, even though I know he can.

He gets to his feet and walks over to me. I don't have a chance to stand before he's in front of me, his hands on each armrest as he leans closer. "I can, and I will, doc. You have everything to lose. I have *nothing*."

A light sweat gathers on my palms. There's nothing scarier than a man with nothing to lose.

"Do you remember the night I left you in your bathroom?" he asks.

I swallow.

"Did you enjoy my come on your cunt the next morning?"

My cheeks flush. I woke up thinking it was my own come from playing with myself because it had mostly soaked into my skin, mixing with my slick excitement.

"Why are you doing this to me?" I lift my gaze to meet his.

His hand brushes my cheek. "Because I'm in love with you. Absolutely *obsessed* with you."

My breath hitches as his lips draw closer to mine. "You can't be."

He smirks. "I no longer want to talk about me at these appointments. I just want to use you. Make up whatever you have to for the court, because I'm done talking."

His lips crash into mine, and my laptop falls to the ground as he lifts me to my feet. The jolt between my legs overpowers my fear, my scruples, and my sanity.

He pushes my shoulders until I'm on my knees. He's so strong. Too strong. He keeps one hand on my shoulder while the other unzips his jeans and frees himself. I didn't see his cock when he had sex with me last week. I only felt the strength behind it as he stretched me. Looking at it now, I don't know how I fit it inside me.

"Suck my dick," he says, shoving his cock past my lips.

My red lipstick smears across the length of his cock as he pulls out before pushing deeper into my mouth. I gag when it collides with the back of my throat. He fucks my mouth until tears roll down my cheeks.

"Good fucking girl," he says as his head drops back.

"Maxim," I whisper as he pulls out of my mouth to let me catch my breath.

"When you say my name like that, it reminds me of how you moaned my name as you pleased yourself," he groans.

"Wh-what?"

"I watched you before I marked your pussy. You said my name while you rubbed yourself. What were you thinking about, doc?"

"I'm not—"

"I think you were thinking about me between your thighs. With my mouth on your little cunt, huh?"

I was. But I don't want to tell him that.

I shake my head, and he slaps my cheek, making me whimper.

"Yes," I say, a drop in my shoulders as I sit back on my heels. I didn't want to give him that validation, but he's drawing it out of me.

"Why didn't you just ask?" he says as he grabs my arm and helps me to my feet. He lifts me and places me on the edge of my desk.

Unethical

"No . . ." I whisper, pushing his hands away as they ride up my thighs, carrying my skirt along with them.

I could never ask him for what I've thought about. It's so wrong. I'd never be able to utter those words out loud. The admission would mean I'm no longer a coerced therapist.

It means I'm an unethical one.

"Shh, doc. You want my mouth on you enough to come to it, so let me make you come."

He drops to his knees and wraps his arms around my thighs as he pulls me toward him. The corner of the desk digs into my ass, but his tongue licks away the pain. He moves my panties aside first, enjoying the taste of my wetness.

The rough motion makes goosebumps rise on my skin. His warm, soft tongue hits my slit and feels better than my mind could imagine. The tip of his tongue curls and flicks against my clit, and I have to shove my hand over my mouth to keep from moaning out loud and alerting my secretary. I'd never be able to explain why a murderous felon is eating me out on my desk, and why it's making me moan like this.

My hand drops to his hair, and I pull him into me, burying him further. He eats me in ways I've never felt, like I'm his favorite meal. *Better* than his favorite meal. My back arches, and my chest rises.

"Maxim," I whimper, and he strokes his dick to his name within my moan.

"Come for me," he growls, vibrating my clit.

I grind against his face, curling my pelvis to give him better access to my clit. It's been so long since I've come the way he's made me come the last two weeks.

He's vile.

Dangerous.

Disgustingly sinful.

He's so good with his mouth that I can almost forget he's a felon. A murderer. A sociopath. But at this moment, the most dangerous thing about him is his skill with my body as he forces me to come on his face.

"Good girl," he growls, sending a flat stroke of his tongue along my entire slit and making my body lurch.

"This is so wrong." I sigh as he stands and leans over me.

"Keep playing with me and you'll start to realize that being wrong feels so much better than always doing what's right, I promise you that."

With his warm cock resting against my pussy, he kisses me, and I feel more guilt with his mouth on my lips than when his head was between my legs. He wrestles with my tongue as much as he does my morals.

He pulls away and looks down at me as he grips his cock and rubs it down my slit before pushing inside me. I moan against his shirt, burying my face in the fabric. His cock stretches me, and the familiar fullness fills me. He pushes to the hilt inside me, my clit grinding along the skin of his pelvis.

I'm so sensitive. My nerves are on fire as he rubs me with every thrust of his hips.

His hand rises and wraps around my throat, his fingertips digging into my neck. "I'm going to worship you, doc. You just need to shut your pretty mouth and let me. I'm going to make you come, fill and mark you as mine, and you're going to fake your notes to the court so I can keep fucking you the way you won't admit you like."

I moan against his harsh words. I can't admit how much I like what he does to me. I can't admit that to *anyone*, including myself. He could ruin my career, take my life when he's done with me, but as he spreads my thighs wider so he can fuck me harder and faster, I can only think of how he's making me feel.

"Don't come inside me," I tell him. His thrusts have grown ragged, and I know he's close.

He moves his hand from my neck to my chin, squeezing roughly. "I will always fill you up, because my sin becomes one with yours when I come inside you."

He fills me with a stutter of his hips, and panic washes over me, just like the first time. Then he pulls out of me and puts my panties back in place.

"Now I want you to finish your day and sit in front of each and every client with my come dripping from you."

And despite how wrong I know it is, I also know I'll do exactly what he wants.

Chapter Twenty-Five

Maxim

Sarah's car rolls up to the stop sign at the end of her road. I'm hidden on the street adjacent to it, watching. Waiting. As soon as I spot her, I start my car and prepare to follow her.

When I'm not in an appointment with her or watching her from outside her home, I'm following her as she goes through her day-to-day activities. What else does someone like me have to do besides obsess?

The same day every week, Sarah goes grocery shopping at the same store at nearly the same time. Every other week, she goes to the dry cleaners with her pretty pencil skirts, dress slacks, and blouses. Same day. Nearly the same time.

This woman is so regimented.

It's really sad, actually, and I can't help wondering if she experienced an ounce of spontaneity in her life before I came along. Since entering the picture, I've obliterated her normalcy. I've infiltrated her job, her home, her sleep, and her routines.

I've infiltrated *her*.

But now that I'm finally getting a molecule of compliance out of her, what do I do about the masked version of me? I created him because I wanted to get closer to her without risk of discovery. Now I can't ever let her find out that we're one and the same.

Sarah pulls into a mall parking lot and slots her car near the entrance to Macy's. This mall is in its death throes, and the large clothing store is one of the few venues left to stand vigil.

I continue past her car, driving up the row, then back down. Vehicles periodically block my view of her, but she eventually gets out of her fancy car and heads inside. I find a parking spot near hers and follow her, of course.

A blast of stale mall air rushes toward me as I enter the building. The scent of perfume mingles with the overwhelming odor of new clothes.

It doesn't take long to find Sarah once I'm inside. She stands in front of a wall of shirts, her delicate hands moving the hangers across the racks as she looks at each tag to find her size. I hang back and observe her as she continues on, and she eventually settles on several shirts and a pair of jeans.

When does she wear jeans? I've never seen it. Maybe I'm fostering a new, more carefree Sarah. She's already ruined her career. Why not say fuck it to her stuffy business attire?

Regardless of the reasons for this shift, I only know that I want to see her in that pair of jeans.

With her clothing selections thrown over her arm, she makes her way toward the fitting rooms. As she passes the lingerie department, she stops and backtracks to a rack with a purple bra-and-panty set. Her fingers caress the fabric, and I'm sure she's imagining how it would feel against her most intimate areas.

Meanwhile, I'm thinking of how it would feel to rip it off her body with my teeth.

She flips a few hangers forward and grabs one off the rack. Who's she planning to wear that for? All her bras and panties are shades of white, gray, and black, so the fact she's chosen something so bright intrigues me.

I hope she doesn't mind wasting money, though, because when she wears them, I'll do more than rip them off with my teeth. I'll steal those panties and bring them home with me so I can inhale her scent until it fades away.

Sarah turns toward the fitting rooms once more, still blissfully unaware of my presence. A hat hangs low over my eyes, but I pull it lower. I can't risk blowing my cover now. Not when I've just come up with a wonderful idea.

I loop around so I can beat her to the fitting rooms, and then I wait in one of the stalls until I hear a curtain slide across its track. After a quick check for feet in the other stalls, I head toward the heels I know belong to her.

I enter the stall and put a hand over Sarah's mouth as I close the curtain behind me. When I'm certain she won't scream, I release her mouth, take off my hat, and hang it from one of the hooks still clinging to life by a single screw.

"Maxim, what are you doing here?" she whispers.

"I was shopping and saw you."

"You just happened to be shopping on the women's side of the store?"

I smirk. By now she should know that following her isn't so farfetched.

"I saw you picked out lingerie," I say. "Put it on for me."

Her eyes go wide. "What? No!"

"I want to see that purple against your skin. Do I need

to strip you and dress you myself? Do you want to be my pretty little doll, doc?"

She just stares at me as if she thinks I won't. Time to prove her wrong.

I reach out, grip the bottom of her shirt, and pull it over her head before she can resist. Her hands fly to my wrists as I reach back to unclip her black bra, but she's hardly fighting me at all, and I'm able to remove it with ease.

When I pull the lacy purple number off the hanger, she takes a sharp breath. I turn her around, make her face one of the three mirrors, and slip her arms through the straps. As I clip it behind her back, her breasts pull together and rise higher.

"Maxim..." she whispers.

"Shh, I'm not done dressing you up."

I unclip her black slacks and slip them down her thighs. She's wearing her full-coverage underwear. How someone can still look this fucking sexy in a pair of granny panties is beyond me, but she makes it happen.

Sarah leans back, her body resting against me as I work those panties off of her too. I help her into the purple lace and bring them up to her waist. They provide much less coverage, and I salivate at the sight of the cuffs of her ass.

She doesn't say anything as I run my fingers through her hair and begin braiding it. She just stares as I cross one strand over the other. I reach the end of the first braid and gesture toward the black hair ties she keeps on her wrist. She hands one to me, and I tie off the end of the first plait before starting on the next.

"Where did you learn to braid hair? Prison?" she asks. There's a surprising lack of sarcasm in her question.

"No, I had a sister in foster care."

Her eyes lock onto mine through the reflection in the mirror.

"Did you—"

"No, doc. I never hurt her."

I run my hands along the braids and brush the tails over her shoulders. She looks sweet, like a perfect doll.

My little toy.

I put my back to the curtain and turn her, grip her head, and pivot her gaze to each of the three mirrors. I make her look at herself. Her muscles tense and tighten as she eyes herself from every angle, the insecurity evident in her eyes.

"Relax. Look at how sexy you are, all dressed up like a sweet little doll instead of my doctor." My hand slides down her lower belly, and I slip my fingers beneath the waistband and discover how wet she is.

She whimpers as I lean down and nip her shoulder, but she doesn't speak.

"I want to make you come," I whisper against her skin. "I want to see your pleasure from every angle."

I slip my fingers into the seam of her pussy, and her clit swells beneath my touch. After rubbing a few circles over that sensitive spot, I push my fingers inside her to gather more of her wetness before circling her clit again.

She closes her eyes.

"Keep those eyes on me," I say into her ear. "Don't look away."

Her eyes open as her pelvis tilts at my words, chasing my touch and giving me more of her. My cock aches for my own pleasure, but that will have to wait. I love watching her dressed up and trembling, and I'm not ready to stop.

I bite her shoulder again, a little harder this time, but it turns to kisses as my lips trail up her neck. She can think what she wants about me, that I'm a hardened criminal with no feelings, but I do have a soft spot. It exists, even if it's only for her.

Her moans grow louder, and I'm forced to cover her mouth with my hand. The last thing I need is for some nosey shopper to fuck this up.

My fingers sink inside her again, and a rush of wetness and heat clamps around them. Keeping a steady rhythm, I stroke within her until her thighs begin to tremble. Her hips buck, showing me the right tempo, and I gladly oblige. I follow her direction and am rewarded with a beautiful visual as her breasts begin to rise and fall with each rapid intake of air.

She's so close.

"I want you to see how pretty you look when you come. No matter where you turn, you'll see your pleasure on your face. And it's all coming from me. You know that, right?"

She nods her head, and I release her mouth.

"Be quiet as you come," I say.

Her lips part and her ass moves against my erection as her orgasm builds. I wrap an arm around her, just beneath her breasts, so that I can support her as she loses herself. She reaches back and clutches my jeans in an iron grip, pressing her weight into me, and I hold her as she opens her mouth in a silent scream when she begins to come.

I stare at the bright flush creeping over her cheeks as I force her to watch every motion of my hand, every tremble of her thighs, and every twitch of her face as she orgasms. I get to see it all too. In every mind-bending angle.

And she's fucking incredible.

As she comes back down, she relaxes against me and closes her eyes. I wish I could see inside her head. What is she feeling? Acceptance? Shame? Or maybe she feels nothing at all right now. Maybe I've given her tired mind a moment of peace.

Sarah doesn't realize it yet, but I do. She's changing me. Maybe not in the ways she hoped, but it's a change, nonetheless. I'll never be a good man, and that's something she'll have to accept, but I could be good to her. Only her.

I rip the tag off the lingerie set and hand it to her as I release her. "Pay for the bra."

She blinks and wobbles on her feet, but then her mind catches up to what I've said. "What about the underwear?"

After looping around her so I can look into her eyes, I drop to my knees and bring her panties down with me. She grips my shoulders and steps out of them without argument, and I look up at her as I bring the lacy fabric to my mouth. I suck and lick the nectar that has gathered there. She's delicious. So fucking sweet.

"These are mine now," I say as I stuff them into my pocket.

She stares down at me and says nothing as she tries to process what just happened.

"Fuck, I'm starving," I say, leaning closer to her soaked pussy. There's no way I'm passing up an opportunity to taste the height of perfection from the source when I'm this close to it, so I slip my tongue out and clean her up.

She jerks and whimpers as I replace her wetness with my saliva. When she's been thoroughly cleaned, I lean over and grab the granny panties she wore into the store and pocket them as well.

"What are you doing?" she whispers. "What am I supposed to wear out of here?"

"You aren't wearing panties when you come to lunch with me."

"I'm not going to lunch with you, Maxim."

Lauren Biel

I love that she thinks she has a choice.

Chapter Twenty-Six

Sarah

I swirl some Thai noodles around a fork as I stare down at the plate. I admire the colors, the size, the texture, anything besides the man sitting across from me. The man who has my panties in his pocket.

"You gonna ignore me when I still have your come on my tongue?"

I look around to be sure no one heard him, but the other diners are blessedly oblivious. For now. "You said I had to go to lunch with you. You didn't say I had to talk to you. I'm not rewarding your behavior, Maxim. You stalked me—again—and took advantage of me in that dressing room."

"Took advantage of you? That's a bit of a stretch. You were wet before I even sank my fingers inside you. You didn't look too taken advantage of when you were whimpering as you came."

He doesn't even lower his voice as he speaks, and heat flushes my cheeks as I drop my face into my hands and hide from the invasive glares of the food court patrons who definitely fucking heard *that*.

"If I talk to you, will you stop talking about that stuff here?"

Maxim smirks, and it's sinfully attractive. That's the problem with him. He's clinically insane but visibly perfect.

"What do you want to talk about, doc?" he asks, and I cringe at having to endure that nickname in public. All I need is for people to connect the dots and realize I'm on a nonconsensual date with a patient.

"What is all this?" I ask through gritted teeth. "What. Is. This?"

"It's cold-blooded obsession. It's the closest I've been to another human. You did that, doc." His smirk widens, and his eyebrow rises.

"The only thing cold-blooded here is you. I haven't been able to do anything for you. I haven't gotten through to you in the slightest."

"That's not true. You've gotten to me plenty. Like a destructive little bug that's infiltrating every structure of my home, you've destroyed the integrity. You've infested it."

"Wow, paint it in a grimmer light, why don't you?"

He leans forward and puts his elbows on the table. "What is this to you, doc?"

"I . . . I, um . . ."

I can't even answer the question. It's fucking stupid, that's what it is.

I should have stopped it by now. I should have thrown him back into prison to rot. But Maxim makes me feel *something*. He makes me feel wanted and, dare I say, special. A murderer like him shouldn't make someone feel any way but horrified and disgusted. Someone like him shouldn't make me shudder against his palm.

But I have. And I probably will again.

And *that's* disgusting and horrifying.

Is coming on a murderer's hand just as sinful as the man who committed the murders in the first place? Especially now that I know what he's done.

I don't know what's worse.

"Listen, Maxim," I finally say after my thoughts have run haywire. "I don't know what this is. You've transformed me into something I simultaneously hate and love."

"I've fucked you like only a felon can," he says, and those words send an unexpected shiver through my body. "But seriously. You like that I stalk you. That I pursue you so goddamn hard. You love that I've learned your body like a blind man learning braille. You're enjoying letting loose and being used and fucked like someone who didn't spend half their life in fucking college to become the woman who's not allowed to come on my dick."

Him explaining what I begrudgingly feel is equally maddening and vindicating. I have *always* done the right thing. I've always sought positive affirmations from my parents, my professors, and my bosses. I strived to be the good girl everyone wanted me to be.

Maybe that's why I'm drawn to the imperfect. The people brave enough to be openly bad. The men and women who don't care how society views them. Maybe I want to shove them into my perfect little box in my mind. Maybe that's why I want so badly to fix them.

Be. Fucking. Good.

Be good, Sarah.

God, this lunch is turning into a mindfuck.

He must have picked up on my silent screaming because he sits up.

"Listen, doc," he says, "I'm not trying to ruin your life. I'm trying to make mine better."

"Can't you see that I want the same thing for you?"

He shakes his head. "No, what you want is to check off some boxes, put me on meds, and make me into a mindless drone. You don't care about who I am or what I've been through. You're just like them."

Now we're getting somewhere. I have to keep him talking. "I'm just like who?"

"Anyone in the system who's taken great pains to chew me up and spit me out. The foster parents. My actual fucking parents. The penal system. Yeah, I was probably born with a few screws loose, but everyone in my life has spent more time loosening them further than trying to tighten them up."

The psychologist in me wants to spit out all the things we're taught to say in this situation. You don't have to remain a product of your environment. You can change your way of thinking. Yadda, yadda, yadda.

Instead, I say what feels right. "I'm sorry so many people have failed you."

He pushes the tray of food away from him. "And people wonder why I've become a demon."

"I don't think you're a demon," I say, though I'm not sure I'm being completely honest. He's pretty fucking evil.

"Yeah, you do. And that's fine." He stands and picks up his half-eaten meal. "Maybe this lunch thing was a bad idea."

Having lunch with a client is definitely a bad idea, but I'm a glutton for punishment today. "Sit down and finish eating. You were the one who came up with this idea to begin with."

"I just wanted more time with you so I could learn more

about you. Sharing dirty details about myself isn't part of that fantasy."

As he walks toward the little row of plastic trash cans, I take a moment to really think about what I'm doing. I, a respected member of the psychology community, am fucking Maxim, a murderous felon who wouldn't know a boundary if it landed on his head. Not only am I fucking him, but I'm actually starting to like him.

And now I'm about to cross a line of my own.

When he returns to the table, I clear my throat. "Why don't we walk around the mall a bit longer? I don't have any plans, and you can take that time to ask me some things about myself."

While I'll gladly spill some of my own tea, I'll only do so in exchange for some of his.

A smirk spreads on his face, and my stomach clenches. This would be easier if he wasn't so goddamn attractive. "I have a better idea. Why don't we head to a scenic spot I know?"

Against my better judgment, I nod and follow him out of the mall.

Chapter Twenty-Seven

Maxim

She looks out of place in my beat-up vehicle, as if she's a flowering tree growing tall in the middle of a garbage dump. Just beauty surrounded by trash and disease.

I drive her to a park I used to visit when I was younger. My foster parents lived a ten-minute walk from here. I'm not even sure if the house has been resurrected or if it remains a crumbling heap of old bones that are eternally haunted by the screams of their foster children.

"Where are we going?" Sarah asks, wringing out her hands in her lap. She picks at her slacks as she looks around.

Her anxiety is eating away at her. Just being around me eats away at her. But maybe underneath that outer layer is the Sarah that she needs to be. That she deserves to be.

"Trove Park," I say. "I used to visit this place a lot when I was growing up."

Her eyes brighten because I've just presented her with a

tidbit of information without forcing her to wrestle it out of me. I wish I could give her more, but it's not easy for me to talk about my past. Bringing her here is a bigger step than she realizes. Or maybe she understands more than I give her credit for.

I pull into a spot at the very end of the parking lot. "I used to ride my rusty bike up here and put it right in that twisted hunk of metal they called a bike rack," I say.

She peers through the windshield as if I've just told her we're approaching the wreckage of the Titanic. It's just an old bike rack to me, but to her, it's a bridge to some inner sanctum I unknowingly revealed.

Aside from a few more rust patches on the swing set and a plastic slide instead of a metal ass-burner, the small playground looks much the same. The oaks towering above everything have even grown a bit themselves. I wonder if they remember me. I cried beneath them enough times, back before I learned of more satisfying ways to deal with my pain.

Three teenagers stand at the head of a nearby path. I can only hope they move along soon, because that's where I want to take Sarah. The path leads to an eye-catching overlook of the city. It's another place I went often as a kid, but I won't tell her that.

I also won't tell her how many times I considered jumping off the rocky edge and ending my suffering. Some things are better kept locked away.

I put the car in park and stare at the teens, waiting for them to move on. The youngest of the three boys separates from the two older kids, backing off and leaning against the No Parking sign. One of the older teens turns and rips the youngest's hat from his head, then throws it to the ground.

Unethical

When the little guy leans down to pick it up, the second teen plants a kick into his ribs, sending him onto his side as he curls up.

Before I can tell myself to mind my own business, my hand is on the door handle and I'm ripping it open.

"Maxim—!" Sarah yells behind me, but I slam the door, cutting her off before she can plead for me to stop.

I walk over to the teens. The young one reminds me of an aged version of my brother, even down to the messy dark hair. I reach toward him.

"Who's this? Your dad?" one of the older teens says.

I turn to him. "I'm not his dad, but if you give your mom a call and have her come by, I could have her calling me daddy."

His cheeks flush, and he puffs on air. Mom jokes worked well for me in my younger days, and they appear to have withstood the test of time.

"Get going before I fuck you up," I snarl.

"You won't do shit," the other older boy hisses, balling his hand into a fist.

Oh, I wish he would. If he hit me, I'd stomp him into the ground.

"I have done so much shit, little boy." I roll up my sleeves. "I'll gladly go back to prison with your blood on my hands, if that's what you want."

The two boys look around, then tuck their tails and take off.

I offer my hand to the young boy again, and he takes it. After I help him to his feet, I place his hat back on his head. "You good?"

"Yeah, I'm fine." He looks around. "Thanks."

I don't know why I felt the need to run over and defend

this kid. Maybe because I wish I'd done more for my brother. Defended him differently. Better.

"You need to pick better friends," I say. "Find people who protect you and watch your back instead of stabbing a knife in it."

The kid nods. "That's my older brother and his friend. They didn't want me to come along."

"Well, maybe listen next time. Some brothers are bad news." I pat his shoulder. "Go on home now, and when you get there, don't tell your parents. Snitching isn't a good look on anyone. Maybe he'll grow out of this mean phase."

As the kid hurries away, I can only hope he's going back to a warm bed and home-cooked meals. I can only hope he has a better life than my brother and I knew.

When I turn around, I spot Sarah standing behind her open door. Her hands clench the rusting top of the window frame, and the look of relief on her face shines bright. I genuinely think she thought I was going to throw hands with a teen.

"I never realized there was this side to you," she says as I approach her.

My shoulders rise in a shrug. "It wasn't anything."

"No, you're right," she says. "It wasn't anything. Maxim, it was *every*thing."

She bites her lip, steps forward, then pulls me into her. Her lips meet mine, and I'm almost too shocked to close my eyes. Who knew I needed to show just a tiny bit of kindness to get in her pants? If I'd known, I would have allowed her to see this side of me sooner.

I kiss her back, pulling her closer to my chest. When I try to pull away to talk, she engulfs my mouth again. She slides down the side of my car, fumbling to find the back door's handle. She opens it, and we pour ourselves into the back seat.

My skin heats with the prospect of being inside her. I've ached for her since the fitting room, but I've wanted her to want me like this since before she even knew I existed.

She moves a pile of clothes off the back seat, mixing the scent of arousal with the smell of cigarettes. My mouth shifts to her neck, nipping the sensitive skin as she continues clearing room. My eyes are closed when she gasps, and before I even open them, I know it's not a sound of pleasure.

And I know what she found.

"You fucking asshole!"

Her words punctuate the stale air, and my eyes fly open. She's holding the mask.

Her face twists and contorts in ways I can't even express —anger and sadness mixed with a hearty dose of betrayal.

"Get away from me! Get the fuck off me!" she snarls.

I ease my weight off of her, and she rushes out through the opposite door. I back out of the car and round the trunk, but she's already striding away with her fists clenched at her sides.

This wasn't supposed to happen. Not when everything was going so well.

I jog to catch up with her, then grip her arm to stop her when she shows no sign of slowing. "Where are you going?"

"I'm going to hitchhike back to my car. And I never want to see you again, Maxim."

"You aren't hitchhiking with the I90 killer out there," I tell her.

"I'll chance it."

I didn't just say that to get her back into the car. It's a genuine concern. The thought of someone harming her and dumping her body on the side of the road is more than I can bear. So I make the only deal I can to ensure her safety.

"Let me take you back to your car. Just let me know that you're safe, and that will be it, doc. You'll never see me again."

Her darkened eyes meet mine. "Fine."

Chapter Twenty-Eight

Sarah

"Doc," Maxim says from the driver's seat, but I shake my head to stop him. Just sitting beside him makes my skin crawl. I don't need him trying to talk to me too.

"Don't, Maxim. People rarely have to sit in such close proximity to a man who assaulted them, so it would be great if you could at least let me sit in silence."

"Suit yourself," he says.

I'm the one who demanded silence, yet I can't stand it. With each breath he takes, he ignites a rage I've never felt. It's insufferable. *He* is insufferable.

How did I ever allow myself to end up in this position? Before he strolled into my office, my life may not have been perfect, but it was better than whatever it's become. This man has broken my trust on a profound level, and I can't wait to send him back to the cage from whence he crawled.

There's just one question eating away at me, and I need the answer before I hammer the final nail into his coffin.

"Why'd you do it?" I ask.

"Do what?"

"Assault me while wearing that mask." My eyes land on the plastic abomination staring at me from the back seat.

"Can't we get past this somehow? I didn't do anything with that mask that you didn't let me do without it."

My gaze wrenches free from the mask and lands on his face. "I let *you*, not whoever you pretended to be. It's not the same thing, even if you're the same person." I inhale. "You betrayed me."

The sun dips low on the horizon, hanging at the edge of the world as it waits for his reply. He takes his time coming up with an answer, but I don't prod him to hurry up. Though I want to know the reason behind his deplorable actions, hearing his voice only drives daggers into my psyche.

"I can't explain why I had to have you like that, but I did," he finally says. "If I'd known I could've had you without the false pretenses, I'd never have needed to be him." His hands tighten on the steering wheel. "Would it change your mind if I told you something about my childhood?"

"I won't be coerced by your core childhood memories, Maxim. Besides, how could I trust that what you say is the truth and not some manipulation tactic?"

His mouth opens and closes as his brain searches for a rebuttal, but he comes up short. It's a bit of a disappointment. Despite what I said, I'd hoped he'd forge ahead and give me something. Not that I would believe anything that comes out of his mouth in this moment of desperation. He's lost me. He has to know that.

After a few more miles of silence, he finds his voice. "I killed my brother, that much is true, but I didn't do it out of malice. When I pushed him down that well, I thought I was doing something good."

While I can't stop my eyes from rolling, I at least have the forethought to look out the window while I do it. He's spinning some concocted tale to sway me, but I'm unmoved.

"Yeah, killing someone is always a good way to solve a problem."

"Sometimes death is better. We didn't have a happy childhood, doc. Our father was a drunk, but he didn't need the alcohol to find a reason to beat us. There were no intermittent breaks of happiness between the bouts of drinking. There was no loving mother to beg him to stop. Hell, she participated or egged it on most of the time."

He shifts in his seat, clearly uncomfortable. With any other person, this would be the point when I would offer some kind word of affirmation or a sympathetic glance to give them the strength to continue. I offer neither to Maxim.

These are likely lies, anyway. This is how people like him operate. Once they're caught with their hand in the proverbial cookie jar, they suddenly become master magicians. If I look closely, I'll easily see the moment the penny changes hands. He won't fool me.

"The beatings weren't the worst part, though," he says. "Our parents put us inside this like . . . unattached basement. They'd throw us into the pit of hell in the middle of the backyard and lock us behind those two gray Bilco doors. And when I say they threw us down there, I mean it in the most literal sense. One time, my brother's leg . . ."

He swallows, unable to continue.

I turn toward him and expect to find crocodile tears brimming in his eyes, but I only see a clenched jaw and a rage-filled stare. He missed his calling as an actor. If I didn't know him and what he's capable of, I'd probably believe him. He's very convincing.

I open my mouth to tell him that's enough, that he doesn't have to keep spinning a tale to try to save his ass, but he keeps going before I can say anything.

"While we were locked in the dark, me and my brother would try to claw our way out. We were starving, cold, and scared." A look of shame colors his face. "Have you ever seen what concrete walls can do to fingernails, doc? Before we managed to sneak some rocks down there, that was all we had to dig with."

"If what you're saying is true, why not run away? Why not report your parents at school?"

He slams his fist against the steering wheel before gripping it again. "Haven't you listened to anything I've said in all the time you've known me? Do you think I didn't try? The system fucking failed us. I reported them multiple times, and my parents were investigated, but they had a believable excuse for every bruise and broken bone."

What he's saying isn't so far-fetched. Children slip through the cracks all the time. But the fact that he'd concoct such a lie based on the horrible truths of so many of America's youths makes my stomach turn. Just when I think he can't go any lower, he plumbs new depths.

"You're sick," I whisper.

"Yeah, maybe you're right. Maybe I'm a sick fuck. But someone infected me. Isn't that what your textbooks say? What I am is a product of what I've been through."

"Not always. Some people are born with this disease of the mind, and no amount of happy childhoods and loving parents can save them from what they'll become."

He pulls the car to a stop at a red light and turns to me. A fire rages behind his eyes, but something else lurks there as well. If it's pain or remorse, he's faking it. "I killed my brother because I thought I was saving him."

I shake my head. I don't fucking believe a word he says. Behind every genuine moment with Maxim resides a tenfold of inauthenticity. Nothing is real where he's concerned.

Not even the feelings I've developed for him.

"You've lied to me all this time, so I'm not sure why you think I should believe you now," I say.

"Fine, then don't."

The light turns green, and he focuses on the road again as he eases the car through the intersection. I fold my arms over my chest as he continues toward the mall. The silence between us is absolutely suffocating, and I can't wait to get a breath of fresh air the moment we get to the parking lot.

He doesn't see the problem with what he's done to me. The mental torment he's put me through as that man in the mask. He witnessed the aftermath in my office, when I was nearly catatonic from one of his assaults. Does he not remember sending me home from my own job because of his selfish actions?

He has to know I can't forgive him for this. Despite forgiving everything else I knew about him, this was too far. Too personal. Maxim has always been a tornado, but for the first time, he's touched down on me. He destroyed me and left me forever changed.

Maxim pulls up beside my car, and I have the door open before he can come to a complete stop.

"Sarah," he says, but I slam the door before he can utter another word. I don't want to hear it. Nothing he can say will assuage this white-hot anger roiling through me.

I scramble to pull my keys from my pocket, and then I get into my car and close the door behind me. I hit the lock button, and the sound is like a death knell as all four doors latch. I drop the back of my head against the headrest and let myself cry because I deserve to. I need to. A piece of me has died, and I need to grieve.

And that's not even the worst part. Maxim can still ruin my life. He can report my unethical behavior and completely decimate the career I've built.

When I open my eyes and look out the window, he's gone. It's just me and this broken version of myself and the decision I have to make, regardless of the consequences. Maxim belongs back in prison, and I'll be the one to put him there. Even though it may cost my career, I'm turning him in the moment I get back to the office on Monday.

Chapter Twenty-Nine

Sarah

The letter burns a hole in my purse. Not literally, but I swear I can smell the smoke in my car. I typed up a recommendation to send Maxim back to prison. In it, I stated he didn't learn a damn thing through therapy. He never tried, and what he did try was full of betrayal as he hid behind a mask.

As soon as I get to my office, I'll send the letter to his parole officer. I'm certain he won't be surprised that Maxim didn't successfully complete his mandated course of therapy. *I'm* not even surprised. All he's done is lie to me. Everything that comes out of his mouth is a lie.

He deserves to go back to prison. He used me. Assaulted me. Took advantage of me. And I hope he rots in jail.

When he learns I'm the one who put him back behind those gates, I hope he gets to feel a fraction of the betrayal I felt when I saw that mask. But no matter what I do, he will never hurt the way I did when I found out what he'd done to me.

I pull into the parking lot at work and take a deep breath. I pull the letter from my purse. I stapled it to the front of his file, and I decide to flip open the manila folder and torture myself one last time by going over his notes.

On the first page, my eyes snag on an underlined address. It's one of Maxim's childhood homes and, based on the dates, it was the house they lived in when his brother died.

Call me a glutton for punishment, but I punch the address into my phone, put the car in reverse, and back out of my parking space.

What I'm doing is absolutely ridiculous. Maxim has proven he's incapable of being honest, and the house probably doesn't even have a detached basement. If nothing else, this little field trip will only reinforce my decision to turn him in.

The GPS brings me to an overgrown lot in the middle of nowhere. The grass stretches past my knees as I step onto the crumbling driveway. There's not much left of the actual house. Only the singed concrete foundation remains.

I walk through a jungle of weeds and debris to get to the backyard. The long grass flattens under my feet, like crop circles left by a foreign invader. Which is an accurate description, I suppose. I don't belong here.

It's difficult to see anything because of the overgrowth. The plants have really taken over back here. Even so, I should be able to spot a fucking set of Bilco doors protruding from the earth. But I see nothing.

I knew he was lying to me. He always lies.

Tired of struggling to find something that isn't there, I

turn to head back to the car when I reach the edge of the property. As I pick my way through the never-ending plants, my foot collides with something solid. A bolt of pain ratchets through my toes, and I curse beneath my breath.

I look down, but the tall grass obscures the object from view. It was probably a large rock, but I squat and spread the blades of grass anyway, ripping some off and tossing the clump to the side. A metal corner comes into view, and I pluck and spread more grass until I see the edge of a rusted door.

I clear away the grass and dirt until I've exposed the basement entrance. The basement is real, but that doesn't mean the rest of his story was an accurate portrayal of events.

There's only one way to know for sure, and the truth waits behind these doors.

I grip the handle on one side and lean back to pry it open. The handle snaps off and sends me onto my ass. Mama didn't raise a fucking quitter, so I stand and try the other side, straining to get it open as I fight against years of rust and dirt. The metal finally releases its death grip, and a puff of stale air rises to greet me.

I peer into the dark hole and shine my phone's flashlight into the shadows. A set of metal stairs lead downward. Considering what happened with the door handle, putting my weight on them isn't the brightest idea, but I see no other option. I have to see what's down there.

Holding my breath, I grip the railing and descend.

Dust filters through the flashlight's glare, and I feel as if I've stepped into a time capsule that wasn't meant to be opened. The floor is dirt, but the walls are made of concrete bricks. Just as Maxim said.

A bucket stands in one corner. I move toward it and can only imagine its purpose all those years ago. The children probably used it as a toilet. Whatever was inside has long since disintegrated, but dark stains run up the sides.

I move the flashlight through the darkness and notice a spot on the far wall that looks different. Stepping closer, I see that dirt has been packed into a large divot in the concrete. I scrape the earth away and find a crude hole about the size of a fist. What looks like a fingernail still rests in the back of the depression.

My hand clamps over my mouth. These boys . . . What Maxim told me was true. At least one of them was locked down in this cellar, and they tried to claw their way out.

Maxim could have told me about this hole in the ground a thousand times, but the impact of seeing it in person carries so much more weight. Unable to stand, I drop to my knees and sob.

What kind of people can do this to their children?

The kind of people who deserved to burn alive in a building, that's who.

A wave of nausea overcomes me, and I turn my head and retch. Maxim killed his brother to save him. He killed his parents to save himself. While murder isn't the answer, it was the only vehicle he could use to escape hell.

That means he's not the horrid monster everyone has made him out to be. Including me.

I can't look at this scene anymore. It feels as if the ghost of Maxim's brother still haunts this dark space. I hurry to my feet and scramble up the stairs, desperate for sunshine and fresh air.

When I emerge from the hole, I'm a shaking, shivering mess. I've been torn in two, and I don't know which half of myself to listen to. On the one hand, Maxim told the truth

Unethical

about his horrific childhood. On the other, he hurt me in a way that is difficult to brush past.

I rush to my car and stare at the file sitting on the passenger seat. It stares back, urging me to make a decision. Do I turn Maxim in, or do I let him remain a free man?

Chapter Thirty

Maxim

With each beat of my heart, I ache for her. The blood in my veins seeks her out. I smell her on every inhale, and every exhale without her is torture to my soul. I'm sick with a terminal disease, and my need for her is killing me.

My love for her is killing me.

That's what will be the death of me. Not the abuse I endured as a child. Not the long hours spent confined to a tiny prison cell. Though I've walked through the fires of hell and come out safe on the other side, this disgusting human emotion will be my downfall.

I never thought I'd feel this ache after my brother passed. After closing off my heart for so long, I never imagined someone would open a fresh wound on a body part that has long since died. When I pushed my brother into the well, it was a final act of love—an emotion I swore I would never allow myself to experience again.

But here we are.

I feel it, and I hate it.

I sit in my car a mere block away from her house. My foot itches to press the gas pedal so that I can glimpse the woman who stole a piece of my heart and stomped on it.

As she should have.

Pushing my brother into the well was an act of love, but what about what I've done to Sarah? Love isn't selfish, and I've been far too selfish where she's concerned. Why is it that I can only realize this now? Why am I only capable of seeing the error of my ways after I've crossed a line into territory I can't come back from?

Wild desire draws me toward her now. If I pull out of this parking lot and go left, I can be at her house in less than three minutes. I can take what I want. Since when have I placed someone's needs above my own?

Not since my brother, and this is the reason why. It hurts too much.

I pull out of the parking lot and make a right turn, heading to a place I never thought I'd see again. Winding roads drag onward as I drive toward the country.

After numerous turns, I finally return to the main road and keep driving. A tall black fence comes into view, with sharp points aimed at the sky at the top of every vertical bar. My car slides through the gates and continues up the perfectly paved road surrounded by well-manicured grass.

By memory, I follow the narrowing curves until I glimpse the smallest headstone jutting from the ground. Our parents refused to pay for something decent, but the funeral home took pity on my brother and donated a small memorial for his burial site.

The sun has begun to set, casting an eerie evening glow over the cemetery. I climb out of my car and sit in the grass in front of the stone. A river rushes nearby, but I can't see it.

Unethical

I only hear the muffled gurgle of water against immovable earth. Flowers, both fake and real, adorn most of the graves, but my brother's space is barren.

I'm sure he feels abandoned. No one visits. No one remembers him.

But that isn't true. I think about him every fucking day, and I know he's at peace.

A grave is such a sad, terrible thing for so many people, but for my brother, it was a gift. If I could have found some other way to save him, I would have. I would have done anything to dry the tears in his eyes or mend his broken body after all the senseless beatings. But I couldn't, so this hole is his sanctuary, even if it doesn't seem like it to anyone else.

Because I'm an asshole, I rise to my knees, lean over, and snatch a carnation off the neighboring headstone. With shaking fingers, I place it on the grass just below his name.

"I'm sorry, Caleb," I say.

I'm not sorry for killing him, though. I'm just sorry I didn't do it sooner.

We wasted too much time trying to get help from the useless adults in our lives, but no one listened. They just nodded and jotted down the lies our parents told to explain away each bruise or medical emergency.

People say children like us slip through the cracks, but maybe we wouldn't if the cracks weren't so wide and unwitnessed. If someone heard our cries for help as we gripped the edge and tried not to fall, maybe we wouldn't have slipped at all.

I get up, brush the dirt from my pants, and head back to my car. A bottle of warm vodka calls my name from beneath a pile of dirty clothes in my trunk. I fish it out, lean against the car, and uncap the bottle so that I can take a long pull from the glass neck.

I was saving this bottle to celebrate my eventual release. I'm not supposed to drink on parole, but none of that matters anymore. Once Sarah turns in a scathing letter detailing my misdeeds, I'll be on my way back to prison.

I was so stupid for thinking I could be anything more than a fucked-up felon. I was delusional for thinking I deserved someone like the doc.

Lukewarm liquor burns away the tightness in my throat. I've never desired to love or be loved, but now that I've had a small taste of it, I feel fucking terrible. The emotional parts of my brain have been turned off for so long that I don't know how to process each scrape of the cogs as they try to break off the rust and begin working again. Maybe the alcohol can turn off those feely parts, because I don't want this.

Any of this.

I don't want feelings, and I don't want her.

My throat opens as I pour more alcohol into my mouth. Vodka can turn off my feelings, but I don't think it will touch my desire for her. Not unless I down the entire thing and die here in the graveyard alongside my brother.

Maybe that isn't such a terrible idea. A psychopath deserves nothing less than death, even if an angel like her could have salvaged me.

She has a decision to make, but so do I. This longing for her won't die until I do. I want to stay away from her and respect what she needs, but I've tethered my yoke to her wagon and I see only one way to break free. But if I'm going to do this, if I'm going to free her and myself, I want to see her one more time.

Unethical

As a light buzz settles over my brain, I slide behind the steering wheel and start the car.

Chapter Thirty-One

Sarah

Today was the longest shift of my life. I was too lost in a dizzying cyclone of emotions to keep my mind on my work or my patients. Hatred and self-loathing swirl around the desire to love someone I shouldn't. I can't love him.

But I fucking do.

I stare at myself in the bathroom mirror. I look like I feel, and I feel like a mess. This should be better than the constant worry that I'm being watched, which once consumed me and coated me in a thick layer of dread, but it's not better. It's so much worse.

I step toward the window and grip the curtains I hung just a few days ago. I feel like I'm losing my mind as I wrench them open and stare into the darkness.

Maybe I *am* going crazy, because I swear I can see a shadow lurking by a large tree. I can't make out any features, just the human-like shape on the grass beside the trunk. Holding my breath, I wait to see if the figure will move. No one can sit still forever. But maybe my mind is playing tricks on me, because the shadow remains as still as stone.

Instead of pulling the curtains closed, I ball the fabric in my fists and rip them down. The tension rod tears paint from the wall as it bends and falls to my feet. Tears sting my eyes. I told him he couldn't come back, that he had to stay away from me. Now he's finally honoring my demands, and I have no one to blame but myself.

Then the shadow moves.

It could be another game my exhausted mind has conjured up, but I'm willing to play. I step back from the window and grip the hem of my shirt, pulling it over my head with slow, deliberate movements—my best attempt at seduction. I go for the bra clasp behind my back and let the straps fall. When I step toward the window, I keep my breasts on display for the man I should hate.

Disappointment washes over me when I realize the shadow is gone. I probably imagined it in the first place.

"Get your shit together," I whisper to myself. "He's not there."

With a sigh, I turn on the shower and wait for the water to warm, then remove my skirt and step beneath the spray. Hot water taps against my body, and I lean against the wall and let it wash over me. Instead of thinking about Maxim's selfish touch, I focus on the beads of water as they hit my skin.

Once I wash my hair and body, I feel a small semblance of comfort, as if I bathed the dirt and decay from me. I wasn't covered in physical dirt, obviously, but my mind is filthy and fucked up.

I turn off the shower and stay inside until the steam dissipates. I open the glass door just enough to slip my arm out and fumble for the towel on the rack. My fingers meet warm metal, so I lean further in case my towel slid down the rack.

A towel pushes into my waiting hand. Almost as if someone held it toward me.

I shake off that thought. Maxim would never offer a towel. He'd just take it away and force me to stand naked in front of him.

I wrap the towel around my body and ease open the door, simultaneously afraid and intrigued by my imaginings. When I step onto the tile floor, there's no one in the bathroom with me. I start to think I imagined the towel thing too, but then footsteps hit the tile floor and my eyes rush to the doorway.

Maxim.

His haunted gaze pierces me, burning a hole through my chest, but his gaze leaves the curves of my breasts and rises to meet my eyes.

"Why were you giving me a show, doc? Aren't you sending me back to jail? Isn't that what that little manilla folder was?"

That means he watched me go into my job.

"You're still stalking me?" I ask.

"I'm watching you. That's all. I think I deserve to know if you're sending me back."

I swallow. "Maxim, listen—"

"Don't give me an excuse. Just tell me the truth. I know I don't deserve it, but I need it."

"I'm trying to! Will you just shut up for a damn minute?" A frustrated exhale leaves my lips when a smirk crosses his face. "I went to your old house. The one you grew up in. Where . . . the incident happened."

The smirk drops, and Maxim's throat bobs, as if even

the mention of his childhood home puts him right back inside that little unattached hole in the ground.

"I bet that got your psychological panties wet," he says. "Did you find what you were looking for?"

"I found the truth."

"And?"

"I saw the cellar. The scratch marks. Everything you told me was the truth."

He swallows. "Okay, so you saw the house of horrors. Now what?"

"I'm sorry I didn't believe you."

"I'm not a very believable guy. And I need to apologize as well. I'm sorry I took advantage of you. I'm sorry for the man in the mask." He takes a deep breath, his eyes never leaving my face. "But I'm not sorry for fucking you or making you come around my fingers. On my cock. On my chin. You were the one good thing I've ever had in my entire life, something I will *never* get close to having again, and I won't apologize for getting to experience that."

A bright blush creeps down my neck and spreads across my chest. Though his apology is wrapped in a narcissistic blanket, it's still an apology. It's still an improvement of character. In some small way, I've made a change. I've impacted his life.

And isn't that all I've ever wanted from him?

I grip the top of my towel and spread the fabric. His eyes finally leave my face and caress every inch of my body with a stare that I'd begun to miss. No one has ever looked at me so intently, with so much desperate need.

He doesn't speak as I drop the towel to my feet. Maxim has little control and so few morals, but he doesn't even take a step toward me.

What is he waiting for?

Chapter Thirty-Two

Maxim

I've never seen anything more beautiful than her hands spreading and dropping that towel. She showed me all of herself by choice, without me coercing her or tricking her.

She *chose* to show herself to me, and I've never wanted anything so badly in my life.

I smirk at her before lifting her and setting her on the vanity countertop. She spreads her legs for me, and I sink my fingers to my knuckles inside of her as I lean over her and kiss her. She kisses me back, though moans tempt her lips.

My fingers slide in and out of her as her inner walls tighten around me. I didn't have to do much to earn her body's forgiveness. It's easy to play her like an instrument with my fingers. If I could only reach her heart the way I reach her G-spot.

Her lips pull from mine and latch onto my shoulder.

She's coming already. I feel it in the way her teeth dig into my skin and the hard tightening of her cunt around me.

"Come for me, doc," I say through gritted teeth.

She bites the shit out of me, as if she wants to eat a piece of me, but I ignore the pain and continue fucking her with my fingers, dragging out the orgasm that doesn't let up until she releases me from her bite. She pants against my skin, her naked chest rising to meet mine.

I pull my hand from her and stuff my fingers into her mouth, sinking them to the back of her throat until she gags. Then I move them down her body and grip her hips. I need her, and I can't wait any longer.

Her hands grip my shirt and pull me closer, and I allow her to stop me from pulling her off the vanity counter. Her warm breath rolls over my skin as she leans toward my ear.

"I need to say something before you fuck me," she says, and I expect an earful of how I'm not worth it. How she doesn't forgive me. How I'm the dirty, diseased dog she kicked from her home.

But then she kisses me and nips at my lower lip.

"I love you, Maxim. As unethical as it is, I fucking love you."

I'm stunned into silence. She's often sweeter after she's come. She's always been that way. More soft and pliable when her body is coming down from an orgasm, long before she remembers who made her come. But I never expected words like that to fall from her lips.

I take a step back and hold the tops of her thighs. She's glistening between her legs, her slit coated in her come. I'd say it back just for the chance to be inside her. To slip past that warm wetness and sink into her pussy.

But I pull my eyes away from what I'm drooling over and raise them to hers.

Unethical

I don't know how to respond to what she's just admitted to me. Love isn't easy for me, and I'm not sure that's what this is. Is love feeling absolutely worthless without her? Like I can't draw a deep breath unless she's near? Is it wanting to give her all of me, revealing the things I never wanted another person to see?

Like my heart, for one. As blackened and soiled as that organ is, I handed it to her anyway and hoped she wouldn't toss it in the garbage where it probably belongs.

The step back changes the features on her face, washing off the confidence to even admit such a thing to me. I don't want to hurt her, so I close the gap again and drag her ass off the counter. She looks up at me, and I try to find that same confidence to admit that I love something I absolutely shouldn't.

I raise my hand to her throat and lift her onto the tips of her toes. She pushes out her lower lip in a sinful pout, and I lean in and bite it.

"If you told me to kill myself right now," I say, "I'd slit my throat while holding you in my arms. I'd bleed for you."

That seems easier than saying what she wants me to say. What *I* want to say. That word is buried so deep down in my diaphragm that I don't know if I can unearth it. I'm fucking trying.

The look on her face tells me that what I've said isn't enough. If she were happier with me dead, I'd do it without hesitation. But this is so much harder. The hesitation is laughably long as I try to admit my feelings. If I didn't love her, it would be easier. Lying is second nature to me.

But no, loving her is the fucking truth.

"What if I can't say it, doc? Is there a diagnosis for that in any of your books?" My hands slide up her body and squeeze her waist.

"I'd say you're a psychopath, Maxim, like I always believed. Psychopaths aren't capable of the same sort of love most of us experience."

I lean toward her mouth. "I am addicted. I am obsessed. But there's something more."

"Love?"

"Yes, in whatever way a psychopath can feel it."

I take her into my arms and walk her toward the bedroom, but that look on her face, that expression that hovers on disappointment, doesn't shift.

I get between her legs and spread them. My mouth crawls across her slit, cleaning all the wetness that's gathered there. I spread her with my tongue and lash her hardened clit. My hands rise to her hips, and I grip them until she whimpers. I eat her, devour her, until she's dripping.

I gather her wetness and paint an L on her chest. I dip my finger again for an O. And again for a V. And then an E.

"You can't read the word I wrote, not with your eyes," I say, "but you can feel it, can't you? The warmth before it cools your skin. You can feel it there. Just my touch radiating from that spot. That's what I feel. I feel the heat. The memory of your touch. It makes me happy in ways I don't deserve."

I dive between her legs and eat her until her thighs tremble against my head. My hands drop from her hips and take residence on her thighs, holding them open as I push her toward her edge again.

"I want to come with you inside me," she pants.

I've never been more willing to oblige a person. I've been aching for her.

Desperate for her.

And the fact she *wants* me inside her and is begging me for it? Nothing could keep me from her.

I climb over her. Her legs wrap around me as I unzip my jeans and pull out my cock. I rest it on her soaked slit. Her heat burns me, but I slide my hips back and push inside her.

Heaven.

Fucking heaven.

The closest I'd ever get to such a place is inside her.

She screams out as her walls stretch to accommodate my girth. I raise my hand to her chest, taking a handful of her perfect breast before pushing my grip to her throat. I keep the weight leaned into my legs as I fuck her with my hand around her neck.

Her hands lock around my wrist, and a moment of worry crosses her face. If she's worried I might kill her, she shouldn't be. To live without her would be intolerable. I just like how she looks beneath me, with my hand around her slim, fragile neck. The power to take her life surges through me, but the thought of doing it makes me sick.

Because I love her too much.

I stop thrusting. All motion ceases. I don't even think I'm breathing.

People like me can fake emotions when prompted. We can mask and say what people want us to say or what we're *supposed* to say in any given situation. When a person is crying, we know we're supposed to ask if they're okay, even if we couldn't care less or don't feel any empathy.

But I wasn't prompted by anyone. She hadn't even said a word about it. That thought came from me. From my own fucked-up little mind.

I thrust again. Hard. Fast. Because I need to drive that emotion into her if I can't say it. She squeezes my dick as her back arches, and she rises against my hand. I put one hand on her lower belly and keep her down on the bed so I can drill her. So I can feel her coming around my dick.

"Maxim!" she screams as her rhythmic spasms speak to my cock.

I release her throat and pull her against me so that she can scream her pleasure into my flesh. I've never felt as close to anyone in my life as I do at this moment.

I come with her as her pussy squeezes the life from my dick. I fill her and stay inside her until my cock softens and I pull out of her. Come drips from her. Mine and hers. I gather it on two of my fingers and stuff it back inside her.

She's mine.

And with my entire being, even if I can't speak the word, I'm hers.

Epilogue

Sarah

The clock ticks beside my head, and I hear every millisecond of time as it passes. It's hard for me to focus on my clients today. I have way too much on my mind.

How can I parade around like an ethical, well-respected therapist when I'll drop to my knees for a client if he so much as slips the zipper down? Well, not just any client.

Only him. Only Maxim.

And as if thinking his name makes him appear like some kind of fucked-up apparition, he materializes in the doorway. His eyes dip to my chest as he comes into my office and takes a seat on the chair across from me.

"Hey, doc," he says as those haunting eyes rise to mine. They hold a whole different meaning now.

"Maxim," I say as I sit in my chair across from him.

His gaze watches my every move. The way I cross my legs. The clipboard as I set it in my lap. My eyes as they meet his.

"I brought you a little snack," he says as he holds a container filled with cantaloupe toward me. "No surprises in it this time."

"Surprises?" I ask, though maybe I don't want to know.

He clears his throat and shakes his head. "We can talk about it later."

I slide a manila folder toward him, and he smirks before he grabs it.

"Is this my sentence?" he asks as his massive fingers rove over the folder.

"Something like that."

He opens it and flips a couple of pages. His eyes track the words as he reads. Those full lips slowly part.

Maxim lets the file slip off his lap, and the sheets of paper documenting his entire criminal history flitter across the floor. As he stands up and steps into me, his legs push my thighs together. He leans over me and grips the arms of the chair. My breath hitches, and he forces the air from my lungs as he kisses me.

"I can't believe you lied for me, doc. A model patient? Made great strides in therapy? Isn't the same person who walked into your office? Doc . . . you know all that is a lie. I've never been a model anything. Not a model child. A model prisoner. And definitely not a model patient."

He lifts his leg and puts it between mine, spreading them. I gasp at his touch, despite the words coming out of his mouth. But he's right. I'm lying for him. I don't have another choice. If I told the truth, he'd be taken from me, and that can't happen. Somehow, I went from trying to change people like him to playing into his deepest, darkest desires.

Probably because his deepest desire is *me*.

"I won't let you go back to prison," I say.

"You're a very bad girl."

"I thought you'd think I was a good one."

"For lying about me? Risking your career for me? Doc, that's a bad and very stupid thing to do."

"Then I'm stupid. I've already risked it all, and it's my choice to keep doing it. You've given me so little choice. Let me have this one."

"If you want to let me ruin your life, then so be it."

My chin rises. "Ruin me, Maxim."

He shoves his hand between my legs, pushing the fabric aside and sinking his fingers inside me. My fingers curl beneath the arms of the chair.

"Oh, doc, I'll fucking ruin you, alright. You'll be broken for any other man. Unable to come the way I make you come. No one can fuck you like I can." His free hand rises to my neck and squeezes. His arm flexes as he slams his fingers into me with every syllable. He punctuates them with a curl of his fingers as he fucks me with them. "Because I live and breathe you, Doctor Sarah Reeves."

"That's unhealthy."

He smirks. "Nothing about this is healthy. Or smart." He lifts me by my throat and bends me over the chair. "Now put those hands on the armrests and let us both be pretty fucking sick."

He spreads my legs with his knee and rips my panties from my body as he unzips his jeans. His familiar cock rubs against my inner thigh before he pushes inside me. The strength of his thrusts moves the chair backward. There's no reservation between each thrust, and he fills me to my limit. He's always pushed me past my limits.

"I can't last with you like this," he groans. "Bent over in the way I've fantasized about so many times. Your perfect ass against me. Your sweet, wet cunt dripping for me." He lifts me and pulls my back against his chest.

I bite the back of my arm to stifle a cry of pleasure as he numbs my mind with each vicious thrust inside me. Though I may be a bad doctor, I'm his good girl, and it's all I want to be.

I am unethical.

But I am his.

Unethical originated as a newsletter short story and became a serial romance novella on Patreon, where Patrons had first access to this story. Prior Spicy Story Sunday novellas include:
Last Mistake (Books2read.com/LastMistake) and *Protect Me* (Books2read.com/ProtectMeNovella).
If you want to join my Patreon, check out patreon.com/laurenbielauthor

If you want more possessive and unhinged MMCs, take the road trip of a lifetime with the Ride or Die romance standalones:
Hitched: Books2read.com/Hitched
Along for the Ride: Books2read.com/MFMHitchhiker
Driving my Obsession: *Books2read.com/DrivingmyObsession*
Across State Lines: Books2read.com/AcrossStateLines
Don't Stop: Books2read.com/Dont-Stop

If you want to stay on the dark side of things but want to

laugh, check out my dark romantic comedy series. Start with *Sinners Retreat*: Books2read.com/SinnersRetreat

Acknowledgments

To my VIP gals (Kimberly, Jessie, Nikita, Lexi, Grace), I'm so thankful for you guys. Love you!

Thank you to my husband for all you do. I love you with all my heart!

Brooke, my editor, thank you for always being an incredible support system for me as you make my books the best they can be!

An incredibly big thank you to my valued Patrons. Your contribution helped make this book happen!

Courtney, Shari, Electrobean, Cris, Tia E, Tori G, Lymarie95, Sarah S, Kat, Amanda T, Tiffany M, Kala R, _____ britneyxO, Suzy A, Tara H, Andie J, Lisa W, Court's Bookshelf, Stacy, Emily S, Sheena E, Queen Ilmaree, SerenaLorraine, Courtney Y, Gini R, Shannan T, Heather C, Kayla F, Charmaine B, Michelle, Karla, Christy P, Cheyanna L, Mickayla F, Dani C, Sandie W, SweetnSourKandy, Kayla T, Arnica S, Karly W, Cassi K, Gumdrop, Maxine T, Kay, Nicholetta88, Vikki S, Lori R, Jessie, Tabitha F, Lindsey S, Erika M, Laura T, Nicole M, Nineette W, Kimberly B, BoneDaddyAshe, Kimberly S, Sammi Rae, Allison B, Chelle, Gabby S, Jennifer H, Jessica G, Samantha R, Sara S, Iesha E, Margaret N, April C,

Amber H, Caitlyn W, Nikki S, Kat De Ann, Inkeddarkreads, Jasmine K, Heather S, Lizzie Borden, CryBaby, Just Jen Here, Mikasa_Kuchiki, Jada W, Briyanna M, Midwest.Kindleworm, Berthie L, Amanda C, Bailey A, YourMomReads, Laura, Eugenia M, bethbetweenthepages, Sharee S, Samantha W, Lourdes G, Kelli T, Shelby F, Lauren P, Mackenzie H, Tiannah B, Wombles, Kristiana B, Vero A, Deani, Amanda C, Brooke O, Ashley P, Mandy G, Courtney P, Lisa A, Leslie W, Jordyn J, DJ Krimmer, Kayla M, Marisa, Jess M, Amber, Tiffany T, Smitty, Anna S, Barrie, Alondra, Alexandria R, Brianne, Leeat, DirtyPanda, Erica W, Ashley T, Jenn C, Annie Pruitt, Anya, Denise S, Heather M, Bonnie F, Anna, Carolina S, Lauren S, Milan B, Pyro, Iris, Tatted Bat, Tamika, Marguerite, Courtney R, Kimberlee A, Jennifer S, StjoReads, Stacy B

Connect with Lauren

Don't miss a thing from Lauren Biel! Check out all of her books, social media connections, and other important information at Campsite.bio/LaurenBielAuthor and LaurenBiel.com

Also by Lauren Biel

To view Lauren Biel's complete list of books, visit: https://laurenbiel.com/laurenbielbooks/

About the Author

Lauren Biel is the author of many dark romance books, with several more titles in the works. When she's not working, she's writing. When she's not writing, she's spending time with her husband, her friends, or her pets. You might also find her on a horseback trail ride or sitting beside a waterfall in Upstate New York. When reading her work, expect the unexpected. To be the first to know about her upcoming titles, please visit www.LaurenBiel.com.

Made in United States
North Haven, CT
26 February 2025